**NOT
THE YEAR
YOU HAD PLANNED**

NOT
THE YEAR
YOU HAD PLANNED

A Positive Self-Help Book for a Cancer Journey

Cathy McCarthy

ashfield
PRESS

Published in 2011 by
ASHFIELD PRESS • DUBLIN • IRELAND

Visit: nottheyearyouhadplanned.wordpress.com

Designed and typeset by SUSAN WAINE
in 11.5 on 13.5 point Quadraat
Printed in Ireland

ISBN: 978-1-901658-80-4

The Publisher acknowledges the generous sponsorship of this publication by Trulife.
For over fifty years, Trulife has dedicated itself to improving life for women who undergo breast surgery
Their mission remains to design a wide selection of the most natural breast forms,
bras and accessories to restore comfort and confidence after breast surgery.
For further information, please visit www.trulife.com

Contents

PART 3

PART 4

APPENDIX I

APPENDIX II

REFERENCES

Acknowledgements

A book such as this one is never the work of just one person. My life was definitely enriched by all the wonderful people who crossed my path during the writing of this book and to those who have contributed both professionally and personally I now wish to say thank you.

To Ashley O'Rourke (Make-Up Artist), Tony Carlin, Christine Courtney, Maeve Garvey, Marie Murphy, Charlotte Coleman-Smith, J. Raftery, Anna Collins (Nutritionist), Deirdre Sexton, Lily McKenna, Atlantic Aromatics, who all contributed to the book.

To Emer Shelley, Helen Peelo, Arminta Wallace, Marie Connelly and Maeve Bancroft.

To Jane Harrison for introducing me to John Davey of Ashfield Press, to my Editor, Judith Elmes and to Susan Waine for her wonderful designs.

To my wonderful daughter Emma, who was always eager to help and had to endure my rather backward computer skills. I thank her for her patience (most of the time).

To Peter, Oscar and Jack for sharing their stories. I hope their inspiration will help other men on their journey.

To those who assisted me during my visits to the various Cancer Support Centres and particularly to Maureen Durcan of the Sligo Support Centre who gave me permission to include the piece, "Seed of Hope" which hangs in their Centre.

To the many other people I have not listed, your input did not go unnoticed and for your help I am truly grateful.

Finally, a very special thank you to my wonderful sister, Claire who was so generous with her time and made a huge contribution to the book

SEED OF HOPE

What seemed to be the end
Proved to be the beginning.
What seemed to be a cause for fear
Proved to be the cause for courage.
What seemed to be defeat
Proved to be victory and
What seemed to be the basis for despair
Proved to be the basis for hope.
Suddenly a wall became a gate and
although we are not able to say
with much clarity or pre-vision
what lies behind that gate,
the tone of all we do and say
on our way to the gate changes
profoundly.

(Anon.)

WHEN I was asked to write this foreword, I got out my favourite notebook. It's the one where I jot down things I come across which inspire me, comfort me or make me laugh out loud. It contains scraps of poetry, quotes, and chunks out of books. But I didn't need to look at those. I just wanted to look at the book itself, because it was a present from Cathy.

Our crazy society has devalued the notion of goodness to such an extent that to describe someone as a 'good' person at once raises doubts in our minds. If they're good, aren't they also a bit pious? Fond of the moral high ground maybe? Not the sort of person, as somebody once observed of St Paul, you'd want to go on holidays with?

Among our group of friends, Cathy is the one who always goes the extra mile. She's the one who remembers the names of babies who've just been born and obscure relatives who haven't been feeling well. She's the one who always makes the phone call or sends the text that says, 'I'm thinking of you'.

At the same time, she's always up for meeting for coffee or a spot of retail therapy. Once, in a highly salubrious fitting-room in a highly salubrious shopping centre, I emerged in an outfit I was sure would transform me into Jackie Onassis. Cathy looked me up and down briefly, and then observed: 'Well, to be honest with you, it's a bit ... gicky'. The somewhat superior sales woman must have wondered why we were giggling like a couple of teenagers.

For all these reasons and for many more, I have no hesitation in recommending this book to anyone who's in a bad place, whether physically or mentally, following a health challenge. I know it has been thoroughly researched and I'm confident that it's thoughtful and caring and gentle. But, more importantly, it's infused from start to finish with – there's that word again – goodness.

I open my notebook at random and come across this quote from the theologian and spiritual writer Richard Rohr. 'I hope you have met ... at least one Kingdom person in your life,' he writes. 'They are surrendered and trustful people. You sense that their life is okay at the core. A Kingdom person lives for what matters, for life in its deepest and lasting sense . . .' Certainly I have met such a person. And when you read this book, you'll meet her too.

ARMINTA WALLACE

Not The Year You Had Planned had an unusual beginning in that two years ago I had no notion of writing a book of this kind and would never have believed I could do it.

It all started when I read an article by Patsey Murphy in The Irish Times Magazine about a lady who had cancer and had started a business for headscarves. Patsey concluded, 'I wish someone would find a solution to the missing eyebrows.' Feeling that I had, I emailed it to Patsey and got an email back from her. She'd had cancer a few years earlier and her eyebrows had never fully grown again. She mentioned that she might do an article on tips for people with cancer sometime. I discussed at length the type of tips that could be included in such an article with a journalist friend, who wondered whether there could be a book in it. I dismissed the idea initially, but a few days later, en route to Enniscorthy, Co. Wexford, I couldn't stop thinking about her suggestion. It wouldn't go away and so an idea was born. Back home, I started putting some ideas down in my notebook. I could not believe how much information I had found myself writing and hence this book.

I had breast cancer in 2007, and underwent surgery, chemotherapy and radiotherapy. During that time, whenever I had a problem, I tried to find a solution to it and in the majority of cases did so, although some with more success than others. Afterwards, I came to know many people who had cancer and would duly pass on to them any tips that I had ... that is what it was about for me, sharing and being in this together.

Then I contacted a friend who has a vast knowledge of books and asked her for some help with ideas. It had been some time since I'd last been in touch with her, and when she emailed me back, she said she'd been thinking about me. Her friend had just been diagnosed with breast cancer and she thought I might be able to help her with some tips.

At the same time, another friend of mine, who is training to be a life coach, told me that she was going to meet a woman who had just finished her treatment for cancer. She was looking for my advice on how to help this woman, having had no personal experience of cancer other than supporting me on my own particular journey.

And so I decided that these three separate but related incidents were all signs for this book to be written. Finally, I told my friend Audrey about my idea but explained that I was still not too sure about it. She looked at me and asked, 'Do you need a lump hammer over the head to convince you that you have to do this?' I knew she was right.

I know that a lot of the things in this book might seem obvious, but I can tell you that when you are in the middle of a cancer journey, what seems obvious in normal times is not always so clear in a crisis. I hope that as you read through the book you will find solace, reassurance, support and the belief that you *can* get through this.

This book is written out of an experience in my life that I never imagined I would encounter, so I write it with the best intentions of trying to help people on the same journey. I wish you hope and light for the way and the best for the future.

PART I

One Step at a Time

To get through the hardest journey,
we need take only one step at a time,
But we must keep on stepping.

— CHINESE SAYING

THERE IS A STRONG POSSIBILITY if you are reading this that you have cancer or know someone who has cancer. How did your journey begin?

It was difficult for me to grasp that I went from being a perfectly healthy person to discovering I had cancer.

The chances are that you found a lump, did not feel well, lost weight or had other symptoms that took you to a doctor in the first place. If the doctor felt you needed more expert advice, he referred you to a consultant. In my own case, I found a lump and went to my G.P., who referred me to the Triple Assessment Clinic in St Vincent's University Hospital in Dublin. I had to wait a week to get an appointment, which is not a long time, and did not worry too much, except on the day before.

On a cold, crisp Monday morning in November I went in to St Vincent's University Hospital for the triple assessment and had to wait until the following Friday to get the results. That was a horrendous week. Even now, I cannot put into actual words how difficult that time is, the waiting. When I returned on the Friday, it was confirmed that I had breast cancer.

The crucial point of what I am trying to get across is that there are various steps along the way and you really have to take one step at a time. You have to go through each stage to get on to the next stage.

The first step is to get over the shock that you have been given a cancer diagnosis. Maybe for the first time in your life, you are staring your own mortality in the face. You have to grieve the loss of your health, particularly if you have been a very healthy person and have now been given a cancer diagnosis. Do whatever you have to do to get through this stage. Don't let anyone tell you not to cry or to just pull yourself together. They can't handle how you feel, but remember that is their problem and not yours. You have to get through this. As Winston Churchill said, 'If you're going through hell, keep going'.

In my case, the next stage were the tests that I had to undertake in order to confirm that the cancer had not spread. I found this stage rather difficult, as it had never occurred to me that this could be a possibility. Call me dumb or naive, but my head did not even go there. So before they would do any surgery, I had to have a PET scan (PET being short for Positron Emission Tomography). Everyone has some form of tests, as each person is different. I have to say here also, I wanted to google, I didn't want to google, but yes, I did google. You get all kinds of information on the web, so be very careful about what you read. Be discerning in what you accept as true. There are a lot of websites that are not reputable and could cause you great distress.

Just three days before my surgery, I had the PET scan. I was terrified, not about the actual test itself, but about what it might tell me. Mind you, when I went into the Blackrock Clinic at seven o'clock on that Monday morning and found myself heading for the dungeons with signs for

nuclear medicine, it did not do much to calm my nerves! I had the test done, and as it turned out, it was no big deal really. The day before my surgery, I got the results that the PET scan was all clear. I hugged the surgeon when he told me. I had my surgery the following day but didn't dread it as much as I had expected, probably because the PET scan being clear had really made me feel so happy.

My surgery went well, without complications, and I made a good recovery. I was able to live my life for the moment, but the next step was hanging over me and I had to wait a few weeks for the chemotherapy to start – another stage on the journey. You have to take each part one step at a time. If you look on your journey in terms of a year, you will get through it but will find it far more difficult. Try to live your life in between. It is not always easy but it can be done because you are stronger than you think and you will find it easier to cope. Just remember too that you may feel very elated after the surgery. I know I did. If you hit a wall, don't despair, that is completely normal. You are over one stage, you feel you are recovering well, and then after a few weeks you know you have to move to the next stage.

But to quote Beth Mende Conny, 'If the future seems overwhelming, remember that it comes one moment at a time'.

Everyone's treatment plan is unique and will vary from person to person. The Multi-Disciplinary Team will make the decision on your diagnosis and particular requirements for chemotherapy and/or radiotherapy.

In January 2008, about two weeks after my surgery, I had an appointment with Professor Crown to discuss my chemotherapy. My husband Billy came along with me. When we went in, Professor Crown explained to me what was going to happen, all very matter of fact. One of the side effects of the drugs used for breast cancer is that you lose your hair. At this time mine was brown with pink highlights at the front. He looked at me and said, 'You will lose your hair. It will grow back, but I can't guarantee it will grow back with the pink highlights.' It certainly lightened the moment.

Some time before I commenced the first stage of my chemotherapy, I was extremely upset one particular evening. My mother has been in a nursing home now for many years with Alzheimer's disease. On that evening, I was worried about how I would feel if she died during my chemotherapy and I couldn't attend her funeral. After I had shed some tears, I resolved that if it happened I would deal with it. There is no point in worrying about something that may never happen. I felt very calm, serene and determined I would not think about it again. I put it behind me and decided to move on to the next stage of my treatment. As I write this, nearly four years later, my mother is still alive. It really taught me a lesson that you have to live in the moment and not worry about the future.

When I started the journey of my chemotherapy, I had six treatments to complete. I had no idea what a chemo room looked like? I knew where the room was located, having already observed it in the area where I went to have my blood tests. The nurses wear wine-coloured uniforms, as distinct from white. I had seen that brown door open and close on many an occasion but had no idea what went on behind it. It was nothing like I had imagined and when I finally entered the room, it was not as daunting as I had expected.

I found the first chemo difficult, because it was completely unknown territory. Those six chemos that I had to complete seemed like a very long journey ahead but keeping to the idea of one step at a time, I decided to look on each chemo as a separate entity and deal with whatever happened. My neighbour Emer gave me a brilliant tip. When I told her one day that I had five chemo sessions left, she replied, 'No, Cathy, you have four and the last one.' When I asked her what she meant, she said that the last one did not count. It worked, in a strange way, to see it like that and helped me to view the whole process through different eyes.

After my third chemotherapy treatment, my sister Claire and I decided to go in to town one Saturday morning, as she wanted to buy an outfit for a wedding. I'd had my chemotherapy on the previous Tuesday and, although I didn't always feel too well on the following weekend, I was determined to go. I met Claire in town and we did a tour of the shops. We did not feel the time slipping by and finally arrived in Pamela Scott's, where she got a beautiful red dress. By this time, probably three hours later, I was not feeling too good. The shop assistant got me a chair and a glass of water. My ashen white face was in total contrast to Claire's dress. She drove me home and I just fell into bed. I'd pushed myself too far, but I did enjoy the shopping and we laugh about it to this day.

Towards the end of my chemotherapy, I had to see the consultant who was taking care of my radiotherapy. I was feeling confident and decided I would go to the appointment on my own. I headed up to the Clinic, which I had passed by on numerous occasions, but had no reason to visit until now. I went in and parked my car. The car park is a nightmare. Then I headed off to find where the consultant had his rooms. Well, you'd need 'sat nav' to find anywhere in this place. I could not make any sense of the signs but eventually found his rooms. The consultant was very matter of fact and told me what was going to happen. I was to have thirty-three sessions of radiotherapy. When I came out, I was a bit desponden, to say the least, and headed for where I thought I'd parked my car but could not find it. At this stage I felt like crying. I eventually found my car and did not feel quite so bad when I met another man with the same problem. I honestly believe the person who designed this car park was never in a situation like me at that moment. I drove out and wondered what I would do next. I guessed that if I went home, I would just feel sorry for myself so I decided to head for Dundrum Shopping Centre, because a bit of retail therapy never hurt anyone. In fact I met a neighbour and we had a chat and coffee. I felt so much better.

When the chemo finally ended, I had a break of about five weeks during which I went to Spain with my son Jack, my friend Helena and her son Chris. We had a marvellous time and it was great to get away. On my return, I started into six and a half weeks of radiotherapy. I was not looking forward to it, but again as each week went by, I was getting nearer to the final stage of my treatment. I worked my day around my radiotherapy and lived life in between. That was the choice I made. I remember someone saying to me during my treatment, 'You have to go through it anyway, so you may as well have the best attitude you can and just get on with it.' Remember that each stage unfolds step by step.

So after telling you how I coped, what are you now going to do? Try not to be too daunted by the road ahead. Remember, the survival rates for cancer are rising all the time. They are continually finding new treatments and cures.

A few helpful tips

- Seek help from family and friends.
- Try to take things day by day. You will be on a roller-coaster with your feelings. Remember you don't have to be strong all the time.
- Focus on how far you've travelled on your journey and how well you have done, rather than on how far you have to go.

What should I do next?

You will probably feel very confused with all the information you will be told in the first few weeks. So what should you do?

- 👍 Slow down and reflect on what you need to do to get through this time.
- 👍 Ask as many questions as you can; it is your life and your body.
- 👍 If you don't understand something, don't spend time worrying about it. Instead, make sure you have it clarified.
- 👍 Take someone with you to doctor's appointments. I feel this is really important, both because you need the support and also because you may not be able to grasp all the information you are given.
- 👍 Speak to the nurses who are part of the medical team.
- 👍 Don't be afraid to ask for help – consider contacting your local Cancer Support Centre.
- 👍 Be kind to yourself.
- 👍 Try to have the right attitude.

I think it is so important to try to live your life as best you can during your treatment. I saw it as a year *in* my life, not a year *out of* my life, as people describe. You cannot wipe out a whole year. In that year, you will learn a lot about yourself; you will grow. Life is far too short. Every year is precious, no matter what it brings. The year or so of your cancer treatment is not the year you had planned, but it is the year you have been given.

Remember... One step at a time, but you must keep on stepping.

Take the first step in faith,
You don't have to see the whole staircase,
Just take the first step.
  — MARTIN LUTHER KING JUNIOR

The doors we open and close each day decide the lives we live.
— FLORA WHITTEMORE

WHEN PEOPLE GET a cancer diagnosis they often feel that they now have limited choices in their life and this can provoke many mixed emotions. When this happens, you may feel out of control. Going through a serious illness is like embarking on a journey with no map or guidelines. It can be very frightening because you have no idea what lies ahead.

From the very beginning you have to choose if you will go down the traditional medical route or if you will choose an alternative path. Personally, I went the traditional medical route because, to be honest, I just would not have had the courage to do it any other way. No one expects that they will get cancer, and it is an awful shock when you hear the news. I chose to put my life into the hands of the doctors, in the belief that they knew what they were doing. In a way that was the only choice I considered.

So how do you feel that you can reclaim some control over the choices that you will make?

You can decide who you are going to tell about your

cancer, and when you will tell them. That is totally in your control. Initially, apart from my family, I chose to tell only my close friends, as I had to sort out in my own head that I had just been given a cancer diagnosis. It is difficult to express how I felt at that time. Some days I was really strong and there were days I thought that this was happening to someone else.

You have the choice in how to deal with talking about your illness. You may wish to talk openly about your cancer. When I became more accustomed to the fact that I had breast cancer, I decided it was good for me to talk about it. It made it more normal and it did help me. I remember my daughter asking me if she could tell her friend that I had cancer. I assured her it was of course ok. I had to remember that she was upset and needed the support of her friends too. I believe that if I had asked her not to talk about it and keep it a secret, it would have made the cancer something to be ashamed of and embarrassed about.

When I went into hospital for my surgery, my husband suggested to people not to visit me. This was a very good idea. I was quite tired for a few days after the surgery and needed to rest. I chose just to have my family and one or two friends visit me. You have that choice too.

I decided from the beginning of the diagnosis of my cancer that I was not going to listen to the news or read the papers. I did not need negativity in my life. I was going to choose what I would watch on TV and listen to on the radio. To this day I still make that choice.

I also decided that I was not going to listen to stories of people who had died from cancer. Just remember there are many different kinds of cancer and yours is unique to you. You do not know anyone's personal history and you should never compare what you have with anyone else's illness. A lady I met during my cancer treatment died. I was upset but, even though she had breast cancer, it was completely different from mine, so you have to be careful not to get too anxious when you hear bad news. There are some people who love to tell you the horror stories. I actually told people I did not want to hear the bad news.

There may be certain people you do not wish to see at this particular time, because they are negative or difficult to be around. I know that this may be hard, but try and put them off until you feel stronger. Remember you do have a choice.

We live in a world of instant communication and most of us are available a lot of the time because we carry mobile phones. If you are taking a rest and do not wish to talk, switch off your phone or at least put it on silent. Be kind to yourself. The person can phone you back. If they are a friend, they will understand.

You have a choice about whether or not you are going to ask for help. If you are the kind of person who is always very strong and independent, you may find this to be rather difficult. But please remember that asking for help is not a sign of weakness. Accepting help may make your life somewhat easier. From my experience, people are willing to help. But, again, it is your choice.

If you are confused, which you will be, ask family or friends to help you make the right choices. When you talk through decisions, it gives you a clearer picture of what you can do and you feel more confident and in control. I know I found it difficult to focus and concentrate and I appreciated the help of my family and close friends to guide me through a difficult time. Remember too: the way you think when you are ill is completely different from how you react when you are in the fullness of your health.

You have very little choice over your treatment plan or when it is going to happen, but, for example, if you are going through chemotherapy, you can plan to do things on the days you feel well. I always felt well for the two days after my chemo, and then had to take it easy for the following three or four days. I had my chemo every three weeks and felt well for most of the second week. I had to be careful around infection, which meant I could not go to over-crowded places, but it didn't stop me from meeting friends for coffee. I was just more careful. For my third week I felt great and would always make plans for that week and have something to look forward to. During my chemo I went to London for a weekend. Everyone told me that my oncologist, Professor Crown, would not allow me to travel abroad. When I asked him if I could travel to London, he replied so quickly 'Yes, you can' that I was left speechless. On your good days make sure you do things that you like and live your life as best you can. You have that choice.

You can choose your attitude. I decided early on that I was going to fight the battle. I actually decided that I had got cancer for some reason, but that I was going to get better. I almost saw it as a challenge. Please do not get the wrong impression; there were tough days, there were dark moments, but I decided to battle through it.

You do have choices, but it is up to you to make those choices. It is within your control.

COPING WITH TREATMENT SIDE-EFFECTS

DRY SKIN ON FACE AND BODY

Unfortunately, dry skin comes with the territory when you are on chemotherapy.

Dry skin can also occur if you are dehydrated. Dry skin occurs when the layers of the skin lose essential oils and moisture.

How to manage dry skin:

- 👍 Recognise when the skin is dry. It will look rough and flaky. It may feel itchy and tight.
- 👍 Drink plenty of water to keep your body hydrated.
- 👍 Avoid personal care products containing perfumes and scents. The chemicals and fragrance in personal care products, such as soaps, cosmetics, body lotions, sprays and moisturisers, can irritate the skin and make it worse. If you feel that any of the products are causing you a problem, stop using them immediately.
- 👍 After a shower, just pat rather than rub yourself dry with a towel. Use a good body moisturiser, as natural as possible, to moisturise the skin. I suggest coconut oil, which is also an excellent solution for cuts. I applied it to cuts on the hand where I had all my nodes removed (this meant there was a risk of infection) and was amazed at how quickly they healed.
- 👍 Use a mild detergent when washing your clothes.
- 👍 When you are washing up or cleaning, use rubber gloves to protect your hands from the many chemicals in cleaning agents.

Use of Oils
I found that the texture of oils was gentle on my skin and easier to apply than creams.

Clarins Huile for Dehydrated Skin was very helpful when the

skin on my face became dry. You can buy it at any Clarins counter. It costs about €42 but if you know of anyone going to the Canaries, it will be approximately half the price.

Bio Oil, available in all pharmacies, serves a variety of purposes. It will cost about €13.

Argan Oil is another oil that I discovered recently. It is organic, can be used on face and body and costs about €20. It is not always easy to locate, but it is available at Nelsons shop in Duke Street, Dublin 2. Phone No. 01-6790451 or through their mail order service – email dublindispensary@nelsons.net. It is also available at Nourish Health shops in Dublin and in some pharmacies around the country.

Trilogy Rosehip Oil is one I have not used but I know of someone who did. It is organic and is available at some pharmacies and all good health stores. It costs €20.

Liz Earle's Superskin Concentrate is a great oil that costs €42 and is also organic.

After I had finished all my treatment, I went for acupuncture where I met Jett, who liked to use natural products and told me that I could make my own 'body' moisturiser with essential oils. She was a real fan of Atlantic Aromatics products, an Irish-based company in County Wicklow. They give very specific guidelines in their brochure on the correct way to mix the oils. There is an Organic Body Oil, which is gentle on your skin. Using a carrier vegetable oil, such as almond, olive oil or jojoba oil, add a number of drops of essential oil before applying it. Massage blends should be between 0.5% and 3%, depending on who is using them and the quantities here are a guideline – for children, the elderly and during pregnancy use 1% or less; for babies use approx. 0.5%. Use the 1% blend initially, to make sure that your skin is suitable to the oils.

10ml *Carrier* –   For 1% blend, add five drops
                    For 2% blend, add ten drops
                    For 3% blend, add fifteen drops

50ml *Carrier* –   For 1% blend, add twenty-five drops
                    For 2% blend, add fifty drops
                    For 3% blend, add seventy-five drops

100ml *Carrier* –   For 1% blend, add fifty drops
                    For 2% blend, add 100 drops
                    For 3% blend, add 150 drops

N.B.There is a wide variety of dropper insert types available; the quantities above are for use with the Atlantic Aromatic dropper bottles.

Coconut Oil

This can be purchased in most health shops, at the Sunday market in Smithfield, Dublin, the Asian market shops (very inexpensively) and from the website *www.TropicalOilsEurope.com*.

Further Use of Oils

I spoke to Christine Courtney of OBUS School of Healing Therapies, Dublin. Christine is an Aromatherapy Tutor and Therapist and if you wish to use essential oils during your treatment, she recommends Lavender, Geranium, Sandalwood and Neroli since these are all supporting to the skin, nervous system and hormonal system and when used correctly have no contraindications for use during cancer treatments. If you are unsure of how these oils can be used, or if there is other advice you would like regarding the use of essential oils, you can email her at *info@obus.ie* and she would be delighted to answer questions on the safe use of essential oils which can be very supportive during this difficult time. Since she teaches abroad, it can sometimes take about two weeks to get a reply, but she will reply to all emails. Just a note, though, it is important to put a subject in the subject box of your email because, if you don't, your email could go into spam and be missed. When your treatment is finished, you can use a wider selection of essential oils.

If you did not wish to use oils on your body, you could vaporise essential oils. Choosing a good blend of essential oils to vaporise can help to keep the house 'bug' free and so lessen the possibility of you picking up infections. They can also be used to help you deal with stress and aid sleep. Christine's choice would be:

For hygiene blend:
3 drops of Pine essential oil
3 drops of Lemongrass essential oil
3 drops of Thyme essential oil

For the sleep blend:
3 drops of Lavender essential oil
3 drops of Sandalwood essential oil
3 drops of Chamomile essential oil

For a de-stress blend:
3 drops of Basil essential oil
3 drops of Lavender essential oil
3 drops of Neroli essential oil

Remember that a professional aromatherapist would be delighted to make a blend just for you, so check out *www.obus.ie* for a national list of aromatherapists trained by OBUS School of Healing Therapies. You can also buy the oils from them. If you mention that you found this information in my book, you will receive a 10% discount.

How to use Essential Oils
Supplied by Christine Courtney, Principal OBUS School of Healing Therapies

Bath
Mix the chosen essential oils in a tablespoon of vegetable oil (e.g. olive oil or grape seed oil). Fill the bath to desired depth and temperature (not too hot). Just before you get in, add the essential oil mix to the bath and stir to mix. Or, even better, just before you get in, rub the mixture onto your body. Relax for at least ten minutes. Make sure to rinse out the bath – use a neat shampoo.

Vaporiser/Burner
Put 5-10 drops of your chosen oil/oils into a burner, add boiling water. Light candle and relax! Remember to keep away from children and dogs with wagging tails!

Body Cream or Oil
Add three drops of essential oils to 10mls of vegetable oil

or fragrance-free body cream (NOT mineral oil or baby oil)... that's fifteen drops of essential oil/s to 50mls of grape seed oil or moisturising body lotion. Mix well and then apply to your skin. This mix should not be used on the face, because the skin on the face is very delicate.

Face Cream

Add one drop of essential oils to 10mls of vegetable oil or fragrance-free body cream (NOT mineral oil or baby oil). That's five drops of essential oil/s to 50mls of grape seed oil or moisturising body lotion. Mix well and then apply to skin.

Quickies!

To have a nice smell in a room, put four drops of essential oil on a tissue and put tissue down behind a warm radiator.

Put two drops of lavender on a tissue and put it in your bra – this will keep you calm all day!

Put three drops of peppermint or ginger oil on a tissue and keep it in the car, to prevent travel sickness.

A word of caution...

There are some treatments for cancer that require that nothing be put on your skin for up to three to four days on either side of the treatment and that applies to essential oils.

HAIR LOSS AND HAIR COLOUR

Hair Loss

There are many studies that show that for many women, losing their hair is worse than losing a breast. That's because you can conceal the loss of a breast, but hair loss is so obvious and apparent.

(MARISA WEISS MD, BREAST ONCOLOGIST, PHILADELPHIA)

Hair loss is very difficult for women and I have heard of those who, before even knowing about their treatment, will ask if they will lose their hair. If you think of how often women go to a hair salon, it gives us an idea of how important hair is to them. The amount of advertising for hair products underlines just how big an industry it is.

My hair fell out about two weeks after my first chemo. You are waiting for this to happen, so when it finally begins to come away in clumps or sits on your pillow, it is a shock but it is also a relief because you have to face the inevitable. Most people would have organised a wig at this stage, if that were their choice. I had already decided to go to Snips in Middle Abbey St, Dublin who specialise in wigs.

I remember my own experience when the remainder of my hair was shaved. I went in to Snips with my sister Claire and my friend Marguerite. I had been in previously to pick out my wig but the day I went in to have it fitted was very different. There was a strange irony about this day. When I was growing up, a beautiful woman called May lived with us. She was like my second mother. May often washed my hair as a child, as a teenager, and even when I left home and returned for weekends. I had all my hair shaved on 20 February, May's birthday. It was a poignant moment and I felt a sense of sadness. Although I didn't feel great, I'd dressed up because I wanted to look well. I was nervous. The hair on the back of my head was falling out, but the front was still intact. I can remember going up the stairs and sitting in the chair where Keith, whom I had met previously, was going to cut my hair. At the time I had pink highlights in the front of my hair and could see them tumbling to the ground. I faced a wall because I knew if I were to sit in front of my sister and friend, I would just burst into tears. It took a long time to get the wig sorted because I was really fussy and feeling very vulnerable. I can remember when it was all over walking down the stairs and feeling awful. I told my friend that I'd like to go straight home and I barely spoke during the whole journey. My daughter was in the house and I told her I wanted to cry. I went straight to bed and did just that. The funny thing was that, as time went by, I came to love my wig, but that day I was devastated.

I had not seen my bald head until I took off the wig that night. My daughter came in to support and share the moment with me as I took it off. It did not look too bad, and my daughter agreed and assured me that I was just worried about the grey bits that were left. I smiled and thought she was probably right. Her comment lightened the moment. The following morning I got up and decided: ok this is it. I will just have to get on with it now. So I put on the wig and looked in the mirror and thought, 'Oh my God, how could my wig have looked so different yesterday?' Guess what? I had the wig on back to front! So when I had the wig sorted and the make-up and coat on, I headed for Dundrum to meet a friend and from that day onwards I never looked back.

Each Tuesday that I went for my chemotherapy, I would meet Professor Crown. One particular Tuesday, after doing his usual routine, he looked at me and asked if I was wearing a wig. I was a bit taken aback and thought to myself, 'You're the guy who told me I was going to lose my hair...' He walked over to me and said something like, 'Your wig is amazing'. It was not what I had expected him to say and was certainly a thumbs up for my wig.

So just some words of advice when you go to pick out your wig. Always bring a friend or family member with you. It is so important to have support. The salon advises you to pick a style and colour similar to your own. Some people see it as an opportunity to do something different, but really it is up to you. I remember one girl telling me that she wanted a wig similar to her own hair because she didn't want people to remark on how different she looked, or not to recognise her. A recent article that I read about choosing a wig suggested picking a colour a bit lighter than your own hair because chemotherapy can change the colouring of your face. It is important to go to a reputable wig salon that has experience because they will be able to advise you, personally, on what your needs are.

The wigs today are amazing. If possible, do not go for a cheap wig because it will look cheap. Remember you will be wearing it for a long time and you want it to look as good as possible. I went for the whole package at Snips and felt it was worth it. They look after your hair afterwards as well. But if you do not have aftercare, there are places you can go to have your colour done – I've listed them for you below.

It took my hair a long time to grow back but that is not the case for everyone. I finished my chemotherapy in May and I went without my wig for the first time the following January. But remember that we are all individual and unique and everyone's hair grows differently.

A Wig with a Difference

A friend of mine bought her wig when she was going through her chemo treatment but never liked it. Her hair came back after her treatment was completed but she had to undergo further treatment, which unfortunately made her hair very thin. She remembered being told about a wig salon in Harrods in London, so when she happened to be going there with her daughters, she rang Vicki Ullah, who owns the wig salon on the fourth floor in Harrods, to make an appointment. She found Vicki to be extremely helpful and she picked a suitable wig ... in fact she bought two wigs. As well as the wigs, my friend also got a loyalty card, which is valid for a year. This card entitles her to a complimentary crème de la mer facial, a complimentary Daniel Sandler makeover and 10% off other treatments. And all for €200. No, not sterling, *euro*. This may not suit everyone, but that is her story.

The website is **www.urbanretreat.co.uk**

There is also a product called a *cushion band*, which can be worn under your wig and makes it more comfortable by reducing pressure on the scalp. It also holds your wig more securely in place. It helps to relieve heat when your wig gets too hot. It is useful if you are wearing a wig during the summer months or if you are going out for a night. You can purchase this from Anna Furlong, New Ross – see list of wig salons for her details. You can also buy this band online at **www.headcovers.com**

WIG STOCKISTS
CORK

Wigs Ireland at Adore
129-130 Oliver Plunkett St., Cork
Tel: 021-427 0031
Email: info@adore.ie
www.adore.ie

Wig Clinic
133 Barrack St., Cork
Tel: 021-431 8468

Wig Clinic
11 Deal Yard, Mallow, Co Cork
Tel: 021-431 8468 / 086 062 1249

Boots Pharmacy,
Wilton Shopping Centre, Cork
Tel: 021-431 8468/086-062 1249
Email: info@wigclinic.com
www.wigclinic.com

Versacchi
6 South Ring Business Park
Kinsale Road, Cork
Tel: 021-496 7400
www.hairloss.ie

Tranquillity
Hair Speciality Clinic
Rochestown Road, Cork
Tel: 021-436 2253
Email: info@hairscalpclinic.com
www.hairscalpclinic.com

Hair Retain
8 South Mall, Cork
Tel: 021-427 6474 / 086 220 2407
Email: info@hairretain.com
www.hairretain.com

DERRY
Hair Affair
86 Duke St.
Waterside
Derry
Tel: 048 7134 3636
Email: seamusgallagher@hotmail.com
www.hairaffairni.com

Galerus Wigs at Oliveen's Salon
24 High Street
Draperstown
Northern Ireland BT45 7AA
Tel: 048 796 28325
Mob: 0044 7775 846325
www.galeruswigs.com

DONEGAL

Patrick Gildea
Church Lane
Letterkenny
Tel: 086-2366004
Email: info@patrickgildea.ie
www.patrickgildea.ie

DUBLIN

Velvet Wig & Hairpiece Specialists
32 Lr. Ormond Quay
Dublin 1
Tel: 01-878 8940 / 878 8667
www.velvetbeauty.ie

Alan & Monica Harrop
Suite 4, Fleet Chambers
22 Fleet Street,
Dublin 2
Tel: 01-671 0911
Email: harropwigs@gmail.com
www.harropwigs.com

Snips
113 Middle Abbey Street, Dublin 1
Tel: 01-873 3251/873 3443
Email: info@snipswigs.ie
www.snipswigs.ie

Evolve Ireland
Unit 1, Seatown Business Campus, Swords
Co. Dublin
Tel: 01-840 0825
www.evolveireland.com

Versacchi
175 Lr. Kimmage Road, Dublin 6W
Tel: 01-490 0570
www.hairloss.ie

Roches Hair Solutions Ltd
153 Lr. Kimmage Road, Dublin 6W
Tel: 01-492 6829
Email: info@roches.ie
www.roches.ie
*Roches are at ARC Cancer Support Centres offering a wig fitting
service every Wednesday in ARC, South Circular Road, Dublin 8
(01-7078880)
and every Friday in ARC, Eccles Street, Dublin 1 (01-8307333).*

Volumize Ireland
9 Greenmount House
Harold's Cross, Dublin 6
Tel: 01-453 2459
Mob: 087-799 6226
Email: info@volumize.ie
www.volumize.ie

Wigwam
15c, St. Stephen's Green Shopping Centre,
(Ground Floor), Dublin 2
Tel: 01-478 1290
Email: Lyndawigwam@hotmail.com
www.wigwam.ie

Wig World
26 St. Mark's Grove
Clondalkin, Dublin 22
Tel: 01-474 4935 / 085-102 9116

Pink Ribbon Wigs and Hair Solutions at Reputations
Hair Design
33 Johnstown Road,
Dun Laoghaire, Co Dublin
Tel: 01-285 1427/236 9857 (Eric, Sharon, Ann)
Email: info@pinkribbonwigs.ie
www.pinkribbonwigs.ie

GALWAY
The Wig Clinic (Miriam Moylette)
34 Newcastle Road,
Galway
Tel: 091-583 638 / 086-838 5097
www.thewigclinic.ie

Wigs at Bellissimo
Galway Retail Park
Headford Road
Galway
Tel: 091-568 555
www.bellissimo.ie

KERRY

Changes Hair & Beauty Salon
97 Church St.
Listowel
Tel: 068 23662

Wig Clinic
(Located in a private suite in Boots Pharmacy)
10/11 Deerpark Estate
Killarney
Tel: 021 431 8468 / 086 300 5806
Email: info@wigclinic.com
www.wigclinic.com

LIMERICK

Bellissimo
Mt. Kenneth Dock Road
Limerick
Tel: 061-317 541
www.bellissimo.ie

Hair Retain
16 Davis Street,
Limerick
Tel: 061-416222 / 086 2202407
www.hairretain.com

Wig Clinic
Boots Pharmacy
4-5 William Street,
Limerick
Tel: 021-431 8468 / 086-3005804

Marbles Hair & Beauty Salon
35 Cruises St
Limerick
Tel: 061-410 955

MAYO
Gruawig, Wig Sales & Aftercare (Louise Killeen)
23 Cashel Park
Castlebar
Tel: 087-225 0704
Email: loulourodgers@yahoo.co.uk

MEATH
Wigs by Rapunzel's
Carrick Street
Kells
Tel: 046-929 3822 / 087 203 6607
Email: annemanuel@eircom.net
www.wigsbyrapunzels.ie

SLIGO
Wigs at Naturelle's Hair Studio
1 Hyde Bridge, Sligo
Tel: 071 914 3030

Marian Dineen's Hair Studio
Unit 3 West Gardens
20-21 High St., Sligo
Tel: 071 914 2266
www.mariandineenhairstudio.com

WATERFORD

Wigs Medical (Bernie Murray)
Viewmount House
Dunmore Road (Opp. Waterford Reg. Hospital)
Waterford
Tel: 051 879 651 / 086 389 7739
Email: Bernie@wigsmedical.com
www.wigsmedical.com

WESTMEATH

MOHH-Salon (Maeve O'Healy-Harte),
Arcadia Centre
Athlone
Tel: 0906-476166
Email: info@mohh.ie

The Wig Clinic (Miriam Moylette)
4 Garden Vale
Athlone
Tel: 0906-49 1716
Mob: 086-8385097
www.thewigclinic.ie

WEXFORD

Wigs at Anna Furlong Hairdressing Salon
53 South Street
New Ross
Co Wexford
Tel: 051 421 287/420 508
Email: annafurlonghairsalon@eircom.net

Other options when not wearing the wig

Some people do not wear a wig, instead opting for scarves, and there are many different kinds on the market. If you are going through your chemotherapy during the summer months, the wig can be very warm on your head and a scarf can be a better option. Personally I did not wear the scarves; instead, I chose to wear baseball caps with sunglasses. I had different hats to match different-coloured outfits. The hats were really comfortable and very easy to wear. If you put a shoulder pad under the top of the hat, it does not look so flat on your head. You can also get fringes and hairpieces to wear with scarves and caps/hats from the wig salons.

Places to buy headwear

Ursula's Headwear,
Athlone, Co. Westmeath
Ursula Hanley
Tel. 09064 75462 / 086 389 9026
Email: hanleyursula@eircom.net
www.headwear.ie

Feel Good Scarves,
Dublin
Catherine O'Sullivan

Tel. 086 021 2686
Email: info@feelgoodscarves.com
www.feelgoodscarves.com

Blue Rose,
Waterford
Tel. 058-60934
Email: info@bluerosewaterford.com
www.bluerosewaterford.com
Blue Rose also does an organic hair colour which you can purchase and apply yourself. Called colour the grey, it costs €21.50, inc. p&p.

Foxrock Fillies
1st Floor
7 Carysfort Avenue (village end)
Blackrock
County Dublin
Tel: 01 2785015
Email: mary@hathire.ie
www.foxrockfillies.ie

AnnaBandana (mail order)
49 Chapel Lane
Great Barr
Birmingham B43 7 BD UK
Tel: 0044 121 357 3654 / 0044 7951 371061
www.annabandana.co.uk

Bohemia Fashions (mail order)
Tel: 0044 1582 750083
www.bohemia-fashions.com

Cold Cap

The Cold Cap System is an additional treatment that is available in tandem with chemotherapy. It acts to cool the scalp and restrict blood circulating in the area and reaching the hair follicles. It is effective in preventing hair loss for most chemotherapy drugs.

Lily McKenna undertook to have this procedure. She explains very clearly the process and her own personal experience.

It consists of a helmet like device containing an insert of liquid that is frozen in advance. This is inserted into the helmet and held in place by a wide chin strap where it makes contact with the scalp. It is maintained at minus 5 degrees. It freezes the scalp, the effect of which is to prevent the chemotherapy from travelling up the hair shaft so it helps retain most of the hair. The cap is applied approximately 45mins to 1 hours in advance of the chemotherapy infusion and again for the same period after the chemotherapy session ends which increases the time spent in the chemotherapy unit.

It is crucial that before the cap is fitted you cover your hair in a good quality conditioner to help keep the hair moist. Hair will thin and there will be some patching but overall the amount of hair retained is excellent. The quality will also change, it will become coarse and the regrowth will be wavy. It is recommended that the hair is only washed once a week, in tepid water, and only use the cool cycle on the hairdryer or preferably do not use a hairdryer. On occasions I washed it twice a week but **never** on the day of treatment, that is very important.

Not everyone can tolerate wearing the Cold Cap as it can feel very cold and can lead to neuralgia or headaches. I am happy to report that I did not have these symptoms, and my experience was very positive. One unpleasant side effect for me after it finished is a slight displacement of the jaw line which causes me to bite down on my tongue at night-time and during the day I feel that my jaw is slightly protruding. Overall I am happy that I used the Cold Cap as my primary objective was to save my hair.

The procedure is not widely available and the patient will have to ask their Oncologist for the information. I strongly recommend that everyone research this as the psychological boost of being able to retain hair will support the patient through the various treatments. It is a very individual choice and you must decide if this is the correct one for you.

This procedure is carried out in the Blackrock Clinic, St. James Hospital and the Mater Hospital. If you are going to undertake this treatment, just check first with your Medical Insurance Provider to clarify that you are covered.

Hair Colour

It is vitally important that wherever you decide to go for your colour, they do a patch test on you. You may have a reaction to hair colour after the chemotherapy and you will know this only when you do a patch test. The day I went in to get my first organic colour, I was excited. I couldn't wait to take off the wig and thought I would look exactly like I did before I lost my hair. That clearly did not happen and I came out very disappointed. My hair was grey and the first colour did not take properly. The second colour was better and by the third colour I was really happy. I remember coming out afterwards and ringing my sister to tell her that I finally felt my hair was back to where it was before my chemotherapy. You have to use organic colour in your hair for at least six months. Make sure that your hair has fully grown back and that you have had it cut a few times ... this makes it grow stronger. I know that some people are tempted to let their hair grow and not have it trimmed but that is not the best course of action. You are advised to have your hair trimmed. You can return to using ordinary colour if you wish, but I have to say I love the organic colour now and find it gentler on my hair. But it is entirely up to you.

Where to go for the organic colour

The company that supplies organic colour to salons around the country is called RJM. When I spoke to John Morrow, he advised me that the best way to find the nearest hair salon stocking his product is to phone 01-617 7960, tell them where you live and they should be able to give you the appropriate name. RJM is introducing new salons to their products all the time. There is also a website *www.organiccoloursystems.com.*

There is another colour product called *NAYO by KEMON* and available through Xpert Professional Haircare. It is organic and used for people who have very sensitive skin. Maeve O'Healy-Harte, a specialist wig stylist at MOHH Athlone, uses it for people whose hair is growing back after chemotherapy. If you are interested in finding out what salons stock this product, you can ring 045-856490/856487 or email sales@xperthair.ie

VILLA LODOLA's VIS Shampoo and Lotion are organic ecological products for delicate hair that lacks strength. VIS shampoo formulation is extremely rich in proteins and essential amino acids that have hair-thickening and hair growth-stimulating properties. VIS Lotion is for topical use, indicated for treating hair loss and stimulating the production of hair. Its formula is packed with active ingredients that add vitality to the hair follicles, strengthen fine hair down to the roots and contribute to blocking hair loss. To check out which salons stock this product, phone 045 856490/856487 or email sales@xperthair.ie

Tip when using organic hair colour

- When you use organic hair colour, always use an organic shampoo and an organic conditioner. You can buy these products usually where you have your hair done. They can often be more expensive, but they will last much longer in the long term.

- The Daniel Field natural hair colour products contain no ammonia or peroxide and can be purchased at Roches Hair Solutions in Dublin (tel. 01 492 6829; email info@hair4u.ie You can also check out the range on line *www.danielfield.com*.

THE MISSING EYEBROWS/EYELASHES

If you have breast cancer, the chemo drugs administered as part of your treatment will result in you losing your hair; that's because one of them, taxotere, will temporarily stop the hair growth. When you're told this, it doesn't occur to you that you will lose your hair everywhere and I mean *everywhere*.

Somehow I did not even consider that this might include my eyebrows and eyelashes. I lost both. I remember looking in the mirror one day towards the end of my chemotherapy and seeing that my eyebrows had become much thinner and that I had just two eyelashes to my name. I was not very happy so set about trying to find a solution to the problem, although I should point out that they grew back in approximately six weeks.

Eyebrows

Your eyebrows are in fact a very important feature of your face. You can buy a kit called *Brow Zings*, a wax and a powder product by Benefit. It involves painting on the eyebrow with the wax and then applying the powder to complete the effect. The kit comes in three shades, light, medium and dark, costs approximately €33 and is available in all the large department stores, including Clerys, Debenhams and Arnotts. It should last for the duration of your chemotherapy. *Brow Box* by Urban Decay is also very suitable, costs €23 and again you'll find Urban Decay products in all the large department stores.

Select a colour that is one to two full shades lighter than your eyebrow hair, to avoid a darker, more unnatural result. If you make a mistake when applying any of the eyebrow applications, erase with a clean, dry cotton bud and begin again.

While doing some research on wigs, I came across another eyebrow kit called *Christian Eyebrows* by Izabelle Hammon, which comes in eight different colours and is water-resistant. I really like it because it contains eyebrow-shaped stencils, thus making it much easier to create an eyebrow and apply the powder. Priced €30, the kit includes three stencil shapes, the powder, a brush and a mirror on the compact. They are available from *b for beauty* in Glenageary, Co. Dublin (Tel. 01 285 1580) who will post out the kit if necessary. You can also order online at *www.izabellehammon.com*

The *Wig Clinic* in Cork does an eyebrow arch made of human hair. They are also available at *Gruawig*, a salon in Westport, where Louise told me that she felt they weren't the solution for eyebrows as most people going through chemotherapy lose them only for a relatively short time. She felt that the eyebrow arch was more appropriate for people with alopecia, but it is a very individual choice.

You can also just use an eyebrow pencil but be careful that you pick the correct colour to suit your skin and hair colouring. Recently I discovered an excellent eyeliner called *Ink for Eyes* by Urban Decay. Available in three shades (black, brown and navy), it is easy to apply and looks very well.

Eyelashes

Eyelashes are much more difficult to fix. I have made several enquiries to find a solution for the missing eyelashes but with less success. You cannot use false lashes, firstly because you have no eyelashes to attach them on to and, secondly, the adhesive is not recommended – your immune system is compromised and you are more susceptible to infection from the glue. You could also pull out real, regrown eyelashes when you remove the fakes. If, like me, you have a dry eye as a side-effect of the chemo, you will not be able to use false eyelashes even if you wanted to. Eyelashes are not just for effect; they actually protect your eyes from dirt and dust. If you have some eyelashes, avoid using waterproof mascara. It is difficult to remove and, again, you could pull out good lashes in the process. And while I was conscious of my missing eyelashes, others did not notice.

Some people have told me that you can use strip lashes on your eyes, which can be purchased at any pharmacy ... not all the time but for a special occasion, perhaps. If you remove them carefully, they can be reapplied on one or two occasions. They're not expensive, approximately €7. But the positive thing in all this is that at least you can easily fix the eyebrows, and that will make a difference to your face.

Check out the American website *Blinkies Eyelashes*,

which was established by a person who wanted to assist those undergoing chemotherapy, had alopecia or had lost their eyelashes from burns.

To help disguise missing eyelashes and eyebrows, you can buy frames with plain glass in Penneys that cost around €2. *Specsavers* and other opticians will also sell you frames in a variety of colours and insert plain glass. They are more expensive but give you a wider choice.

Look Good Feel Better Programme

The Irish Cancer Society runs a programme called *Look Good Feel Better* where make up artists show you how to apply make-up during your cancer treatment. The programme accommodates twelve people at a time and runs for a full afternoon. It is an opportunity to meet other women who are going through treatment.

When I was going through my treatment, I attended one of the programmes and really enjoyed it. There is a very relaxed atmosphere, and everyone is happy to be there. It is a few years since I attended so I spoke to Robin who also took part in the programme recently.

I have to point out that Robin's first response was that she is not really 'into makeup' but she said she thoroughly enjoyed the afternoon on the programme. There were 12 women there, some going through chemotherapy and others who had finished treatment. Robin had breast cancer, had lost her hair and was wearing a wig. One of the ladies giving the programme invited anyone who was wearing a wig to remove it if that made them feel more comfortable. Instantly Robin felt very safe and in fact took off her wig. The make up artists were very sensitive in helping people to apply their make-up. They were shown how to apply make up and those who had lost their eyebrows were given tips on how to apply liner. Each person was given a kit bag complete with make up.

The whole experience was a fun time with other women. It was a pleasant treat and a change from having to go for chemotherapy. There was also a break and a cup of tea. An unexpected outcome for Robin was that she now meets some of the women who were on the programme for coffee and they are a support to each other. She would highly recommend the programme.

The Look Good Feel Better Programme is an American concept. They have a very good website with many useful tips. Have a look at it. It is www.lookgoodfeelbetter.org.

The Programme is held in all the major hospitals in Ireland: Beaumont Hospital, St Vincent's Hospital, Tallaght Hospital, St Luke's Hospital, Galway Regional, Cork University Hospital, Letterkenny Hospital, St James's Hospital, Mayo General Hospital and Waterford Regional Hospital.

If you would like to take part, you should make enquiries at the hospital you attend for your treatment.

NAIL CARE

Some chemotherapy drugs can damage your nails. On my fourth chemo, my nails began to deteriorate, breaking halfway down the nail. Some people's nails go black. There is not much you can do to arrest this situation but here are some tips, which should help:

- Always wear gloves when washing the dishes or gardening, particularly if you have had your lymph nodes removed. You do not want to get cuts when in the garden because this could cause infection.
- If you are going for a manicure during chemotherapy – that is, if you have no problem with your nails – it is a good idea to bring your own manicure set so as to avoid infection.

👍 Ask the manicurist to push back the cuticles but not to cut them.

👍 Do not use artificial nails. They are made of plastic and are glued onto the nail plate. The artificial nails can lift. If water gets in between the nail plate and the artificial nail, bacteria will breed and the water will soften the nail plate, allowing the bacteria to eat their way through to the nail bed. Infection can set in and this is not advised if you are on chemotherapy. (From *Cosmetics Unmasked*)

👍 Do not use an acetone-based nail polish remover.

👍 Use cuticle cream or olive oil to help prevent dryness.

👍 Do not use hand creams that contain alpha hydroxy or beta hydroxy acids.

👍 Do not use nail polish that contains formaldehyde. Acquarella is a water-based, non-toxic nail polish. It is available in a wide variety of colours. Check out *www.Acquarellapolish.com*

👍 When your nails are growing back, the neem oil in the *Dr Hauschka* range will really promote nail growth. However, it is expensive, so you could also use plain olive or almond oil, which is very reasonable to purchase at any pharmacy.

I CAN'T SLEEP

It was a great shock to me when I was first diagnosed with cancer and I found it very difficult to sleep. I struggled through this time and often not very well. It did not occur to me that I could possibly do something about it.

A few weeks after my surgery, I began my chemotherapy. Again I found sleep difficult and would lie awake until the early hours of the morning. On my second dose of chemotherapy, the nurse asked me how I was sleeping and when I said not very well, she suggested that I take a sleeping tablet. Initially I resisted but my sister, who is a nurse, convinced me otherwise. She encouraged me to take one for the moment, saying that this was just temporary and it would pass. Of course she was right. It does pass and in time you will have no need for one. At the time, you cannot see that and you often feel a failure if you have to resort to sleeping tablets. Forget it; take them. Remember that things always seem so much worse if you do not get your sleep; you can become despondent and feel lethargic. Sleep and rest are very necessary for healing during the chemotherapy. I know that when I am tired I am quite negative and everything seems more daunting.

Just a few tips on taking sleeping tablets. If you don't want to take one every night, take one every second night. I often just took a half tablet if I felt I did not need a full one. But either way, however you work it out, take them; the time will come when you won't need them. When you are off all the treatment, which seems a long time away when you are going through it, you will not have the need for sleeping tablets any more.

If, however, you are totally against sleeping tablets, consider trying the alternative route. There are a few products on the market, that might help you. *The Body Shop* sells a sleep remedy called *Sleep Well* which I have used and found it worked, albeit at a time when I was under far less stress than when going through cancer. But if you wish to try it, it is worth a go. The Origins range includes a product called *Sensor Therapy-Peace of Mind* that I have also tried and found to help. It was relaxing and has a pleasant scent. Rescue Remedy's *Night Remedy* worked for me on the first night that I took it but not so well on the following night, but again it may work for you. Tisserand also does a natural sleep remedy called *Sleep*, which is available in health shops.

Some Suggestions

- 👍 Don't eat a heavy meal before going to bed.
- 👍 Try not to drink too much liquid as it might cause you to wake up to go to the loo.
- 👍 Don't watch a programme on TV that will keep your mind active when you're ready for bed.
- 👍 Try not to sleep for too long during the day as this may prevent you from being able to sleep when you go to bed at night.
- 👍 Try to get some exercise during the day.
- 👍 Listening to music may help lull you to sleep.
- 👍 Meditate to relax your mind.
- 👍 Wear loose-fitting clothes for comfort.

These suggestions are all worth exploring and eventually you will find what works best for you.

GO WITH THE BAD DAYS

I learned that staying positive doesn't mean slapping a smile on your face and pretending you're not hurting or scared. It means being kind to yourself, accepting your feelings and then finding ways to feel better.

—DOMINI STUART

You are going to experience a range of feelings during your treatment. Apart from anything else, the treatment will make you feel unwell, which in turn will affect your mood. So what do you do?

Go with the bad days. Feel how you feel, don't try to deny or hide it. I know it is difficult, but it is the only way through it. If you are having a bad day and are told by someone to be positive, please do not listen to them, since they truly do not know what they are saying to you. If you are feeling particularly awful, scared or frightened, it does not mean that you are not positive. In fact, staying positive means accepting how you feel, going with the bad days and trying to find ways to feel better. I remember very vividly one particular evening when I was feeling dreadful. My sister Claire had called in and we were planning to watch the DVD *Enchanted* with my daughter, Emma. I went to bed for a rest and stayed there for some time. Eventually something motivated me to get up again, although I was by then 99% sure I was going to stay in bed. I went downstairs, had my dinner, watched the DVD with Claire and Emma and even went for a short walk with my husband. And you know what? I felt great afterwards. I had been so close to giving in that evening, but because I went with how I felt, I was able to get up later and rise above it.

I believe that if you allow yourself to feel down and stay with those feelings, it is easier to come up again. Denying it is not the solution and not being fair to yourself. If a child is sick, what does it need? It needs hugs and plenty of TLC. Well that is exactly what you need on your bad days. You just need some sympathy so please be gentle on yourself. It is perfectly ok to hide away from the world on those days you feel dreadful; there are other days when you are more positive and wish to be with people.

There are times you can accept your cancer, and there are times when you ask yourself, why did I get this? All these feelings are normal. It is very difficult, in fact impossible, to feel positive all the time. You will have days that are truly awful but you will have some great days. On the good days, you really appreciate the feeling of wellness.

Tips for the bad days

- 👍 Watch your favourite DVD
- 👍 Listen to music
- 👍 Talk to a friend
- 👍 Go for a walk
- 👍 Eat that bar of chocolate
- 👍 Have a glass of wine, maybe two or even the bottle, although I am not responsible for how you might feel afterwards!

Just do whatever gets you through it. I met a friend recently called Fiona who talked to me about how she coped with the bad days. She used visualisation. She told me what you think affects your emotions and this in turn affects how you feel. To quote John O'Donohue:

> Steady yourself and see
> That it is your own thinking
> That darkens your world ....

Fiona received some greeting cards from friends during her treatment. She would stand a card up and really look at it. Some were of flowers, a beautiful scene or children. In her mind she would recall these images and they took her to a peaceful place. She would spend time just focusing on the image she had chosen. The visualisation changed her thinking, which in turn changed how she felt. When ill in hospital at one stage during her treatment, she used visualisation very successfully.

Our imaginative mind can take us anywhere we want to go. Children are wonderful in their imagination but, as adults, we seem to lose the ability to be creative. Our thoughts, both good and bad, are very powerful and we don't always realise their effect on our lives. Take chemotherapy, for example. You can look on it as a toxic drug, which of course it is, but if you believe that these drugs are going to help in your recovery and in preventing the cancer from returning, you can turn the whole thing on its head. The drugs may make you sick, but in the long term they are going to make you well. Think about it! If you were to say to yourself every day, 'I am going to be well', this is a very powerful affirmation. Believe too in what you are saying.

To create a visualisation space

One of the first things you should do when you start to use creative visualisation is to develop a sanctuary within yourself where you can go to whenever you wish.

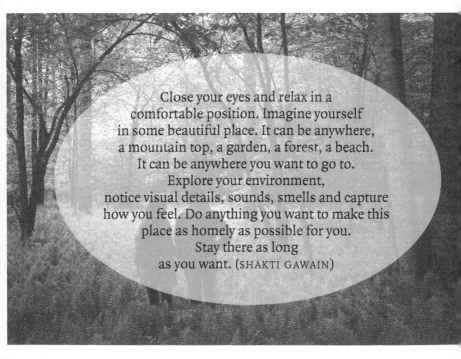

Close your eyes and relax in a
comfortable position. Imagine yourself
in some beautiful place. It can be anywhere,
a mountain top, a garden, a forest, a beach.
It can be anywhere you want to go to.
Explore your environment,
notice visual details, sounds, smells and capture
how you feel. Do anything you want to make this
place as homely as possible for you.
Stay there as long
as you want. (SHAKTI GAWAIN)

From now on you can return to this space at any time by closing your eyes and wishing to be there. It is a special place of healing for you. Just remember this place can bring you peace and tranquillity. A good website for relaxation techniques for stress relief is   http://www.helpguide.org/mental/stress_relief_meditation_yoga_relaxation.htm It provides advise and tips on different methods and I found is very user friendly.

Instead of seeing the rug being pulled from under us,
We can learn to dance on the shifting carpet.
(THOMAS CRUM)

When we experience pure silence in the mind, the body becomes silent also. And in that field of silence, healing is much more efficient.
(DEEPAK CHOPRA)

CHEMO BRAIN

When I was given the facts about some of the side effects of the chemotherapy, I was made aware that I would lose my hair but no one ever told me that I would also lose my brain. I jest of course. I did not actually *lose* my brain, although it felt like it sometimes, but I did have the effects of a condition called Chemo Brain. It is difficult to explain and harder for someone else to understand. I would describe myself as being 'all over the place', forgetting names, losing my keys and being distracted. I could not read a book, because I could not concentrate. This is how Fred Hutchinson of the Cancer Research Centre explains it:

The condition encompasses a range of problems much like those linked to aging. Patients cannot remember where they put their keys or recall lists of things they had planned to accomplish. Some say they are easily distracted or lose the ability to calculate in their heads.

Survivors report diminished quality of life and daily functioning, and the impairment comes at economic, emotional and interpersonal costs.

It is difficult to gauge the prevalence of chemo brain. While researchers will agree that its occurrence depends on the type of treatment, rather than on the type of cancer, there is little known as to who is more likely to suffer from it or who is more probable to have long-term effects. High doses of chemotherapy can have side effects.

How did chemo brain affect me?

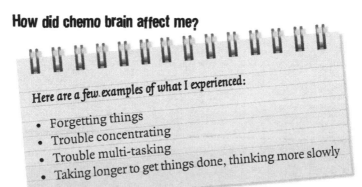

Here are a few examples of what I experienced:

- Forgetting things
- Trouble concentrating
- Trouble multi-tasking
- Taking longer to get things done, thinking more slowly

It is helpful to be aware of chemo brain because you won't blame yourself or feel frustrated if you lose things. Very often you don't even know what is happening; and are not aware of this being a problem until someone tells you about the condition.

Is chemo brain real?

Yes, chemo brain is real and affects both men and women. Its cause is unknown. It could be caused by any of the following factors:

- The stress of the cancer itself
- Low blood counts
- Tiredness / fatigue
- Chemo drugs
- Sleep problems
- Anxiety / depression

What can I do to manage chemo brain?

👍 Use a daily planner. Write everything down and make lists of things you have to do, such as appointments to remember and something that is important in your life right now.

👍 Use your brain. Do crosswords and puzzles, or anything that will keep your brain active.

👍 Get enough sleep and rest.

👍 Exercise your body. Physical exercise is good for the mind and body.

👍 Eat healthy food.

👍 Try and be mindful of where you put things.

👍 Focus on doing one thing at a time, don't multi-task.

👍 Do not be hard on yourself. Try not to focus too much on how these symptoms are bothering you. If you are aware of the problem and accept it, it is easier to deal with it. I am sure that people don't notice it as much as you do.

Of course, we all forget things from time, even if we were never on chemotherapy. To be honest, there were times that I just had to laugh at some of the things I would forget. In my own experience it was short term and now, some years later, I wonder if it was a combination of factors, such as worry and anxiety over my illness which, contributed to this. That is not to minimise chemo brain or to say that it does not exist.

FATIGUE

Fatigue is often confused with tiredness. There is a difference. We all get tired. We usually know why we are tired and a good night's sleep will solve the problem. Fatigue is a daily lack of energy. It is an unusual or excessive tiredness and it is not relieved by sleep. It can last a month, six months or longer, depending on the cause. It can have a serious negative impact on a person's life and on their ability to cope.

Fatigue is common during cancer treatment. It can occur after the surgery, or during chemotherapy and radiotherapy. It can be as a result of the cancer or the effects of the treatment. If you have had surgery, it may take a while to recover. The chemotherapy drugs may leave your energy levels depleted. The radiotherapy can also make you very tired, but the tiredness here could also be the result of having to travel to and from your treatment.

What causes fatigue in cancer patients?

The chemotherapy can cause fatigue. You may not suffer from tiredness after the first few treatments of chemotherapy, but some people find that the chemotherapy effects can be cumulative (fatigue that increases over time) and as the treatments progress they feel more tired. This is not always the case for everyone, of course. Personally I did not feel overwhelmed by tiredness when I was having my chemotherapy, although there were times when I did have to rest and take it easy.

Radiotherapy can also cause fatigue. Some people find that as the treatment progresses, they can become more tired. I did not feel too tired, but one of the big advantages for me was I lived very close to where I had my radiotherapy. As I have said, patients don't always know if the tiredness is a result of the treatment or a combination of the treatment and the associated travel at the same time.

Cancer treatments can cause reduced blood counts, which could lead to a person being anaemic. Anaemia can result in fatigue.

If a person has to take medication for nausea, pain, depression or anxiety, the medication can make you tired.

It is also well known that chronic pain can cause fatigue. If you are in a lot of pain, you may find sleep difficult, which in turn may cause weariness.

You can also become exhausted if you're feeling stressed or worried. I know that when I was first diagnosed, I was very anxious, could not sleep and could not eat. I was more tired than usual. Anxiety is also caused by fear of the unknown.

If you feel depressed or low in your mood, you can also feel that your energy levels are depleted. You may find that those things you would have done without a thought previously are now burdensome.

What can you do?

- Try to accept your fatigue. The more you fight against it, the more frustrated you will feel.
- Try to pace yourself. You may find that if you go out in the morning for shopping or to meet a friend, you may have to rest in the afternoon.
- Assess what are the times of the day when you feel most tired. This will help you to plan your time better.
- Fatigue symptoms include irritability, nervousness, anxiety, impatience, lack of energy, sleepiness and feeling weak. If you experience any of these, accept that you are tired. Being aware of and knowing your own body does help.
- Before you got ill, you may have been able to multi-task, but now you may have to accept that you will have to go at a slower pace. Do one thing at a time.
- Decide what is important and has to be done. Do not waste energy on things that could be done at a later date.
- Try to exercise. If you can, go out for a walk; it can make you feel better.
- Accept help.

Looking back, I can remember one thing that I found extremely helpful. Both my older children, David and Emma, were able to drive and if I needed to go somewhere they would offer to take me. This was a great bonus as you use a lot of energy concentrating on driving, being in traffic and trying to find a parking space.

DVD on fatigue

Dr Sonya Collier, Principal Clinical Psychologist at St and James's Hospital in Dublin, with her colleague Dr. Annemarie O'Dwyer, have produced a DVD on fatigue. The DVD is for people who are six months over their treatment and is part of a self-help programme for persistent cancer-related fatigue. The consultants at St James's Hospital and all the centres of excellence are aware of this DVD. If you have a problem obtaining it, you can phone 01 410 3457.

RADIATION

The vast majority of people who go through cancer have to undergo radiation. This is often the final stage of your cancer journey.

My own radiation treatment followed my surgery and chemotherapy. I had to go for radiation treatment for six and a half weeks – thirty-three sessions. I went every day, five days a week. In many respects, I was very lucky to have been able to do my radiotherapy at the Beacon Hospital, which was about a ten-minute drive from where I lived. Many people have to drive very long distances for a treatment that takes about ten minutes. I met people who had come from Cork, staying in Dublin during the week and returning home for the weekend.

While the actual treatment is short, you have to be around for about six weeks. There are side-effects, but just remember that these vary from person to person. Tiredness can be one such side-effect, but, as previously stated, this can be due to the radiation itself or to the travelling involved. The radiated area may become red, your skin can burn and you can also get itching. It is very important to keep the area moisturised. One cream that is recommended is E45. Use it quite generously. Aloe Vera jelly, which is a totally natural product, is also a good choice.

If you are receiving the radiation as a result of breast cancer, make sure that you use only a crystal deodorant. You may get this from the hospital where you are attending or you can buy it in a health shop.

The night before I started my radiation, I picked up a book lying on my locker. As I flicked through it, I came across some words, which I have adapted here to reflect my interpretation of them. These words assisted me enormously during my treatment because they helped me to see radiation in such a different light and made me feel so different about the radiation treatment that I was about to start.

I see radiation as a golden beam of healing light and energy.

Tips for radiation

👍 If the radiation is on the breast, and if you experience soreness, wear loose clothing. Cotton is a soft and comfortable fabric to tolerate.

👍 Aqueous cream is good to wash the radiated area with.

👍 Do not use scented soaps.

👍 Wet two or three washcloths and wring them out. Keep them in the fridge in a zip lock bag so that they will be readily available to cool the area if needed.

👍 A solution for burning, used in Cork University Hospital, is to squirt sterile salt water on to sterile gauze and apply it to the burnt area for ten minutes, three times a day. You can buy the sterile salt water and the gauge in a pharmacy.

👍 A similar solution that originated in Sweden is to make up a jug of camomile tea, allow it cool, and then apply it to the burnt area with sterile gauze for ten minutes three times a day. The camomile has to be boiled to be effective, but make sure that the tea has cooled thoroughly before applying it to the skin.

👍 If you have underarm hair and wish to shave it, make sure you do so before your radiation commences.

👍 Don't ever attempt to remove the tattoos or skin markings that have been marked out for your radiation treatment as they are there for the purpose of your treatment and will fade over time.

Just a tip on where you have your radiotherapy. I had mine in the Beacon Hospital but hadn't realised I could have my treatment there until someone pointed it out to me. The Beacon accepts people who have Plan B/VHI. It seems that entitlements under different plans change frequently. Quinn Direct covers treatment in the Hermitage. With certain plans, Aviva covers treatment in the Beacon, Hermitage and Whitfield. If you have medical insurance, make sure that you ask your insurer if your particular plan covers radiotherapy in the private hospitals.

SUN CARE

"It's in, it's out, it's good, it's bad … In one breath we're warned that exposure to UV [ultraviolet] light increases our risk of cancer; in the next that we need the sun to help our bodies make beneficial Vitamin D. And then there's the argument that sun preparations themselves could be risky. So what's the truth?" (*Green Beauty Bible*)

Well, firstly, the sun is good for us. As well as making you feel good, it allows your body to produce Vitamin D. But you don't need to stay in the sun for hours to produce Vitamin D; just 10 to 15 minutes of bright sunlight (not noon day heat) on unprotected skin is sufficient. If you are outside a lot, you will get plenty of sunlight even when wearing a sunscreen because no product blocks 100 per cent of ultraviolet light. That is the good news, but the bad news is that UV light from the sun causes skin damage.

There is much debate today over the safety and effectiveness of the different types of sun protection products. The two choices of sun products are:

Chemical sunscreens or filters, which absorb the UV radiation and turn it into supposedly harmless thermal energy.

Physical barriers or blocks, usually based on the minerals titanium dioxide and zinc oxide, which in their natural state reflect UV light away from the skin.

The Environmental Working Group (EWG) in the United States, a lobby group that campaigns for safe cosmetics, has this to say on the ingredients in sun creams:

"Avoid the sunscreen chemical oxybenzone, a synthetic estrogen that penetrates the skin and contaminates the body. Look for active ingredients zinc, titanium, avobenzone or Mexoryl SX. These substances protect skin from harmful UV radiation and remain on the skin, with little if any penetrating into the body. Also, skip sunscreens with insect repellent – if you need bug spray, buy it separately and apply it first."

The EWG's sunscreen database rates the safety of a large number of products with Sun Protection Factor (SPF), including about 500 sunscreens for the beach and sports. You can check this out on *www.ewg.org*. They rate products highly that provide good protection, but contain ingredients that have fewer health concerns, when they are absorbed in the body.

What are the recommended sun creams?

Green People Edelweiss Sun Lotion SPF15 is water resistant and available from Nelsons Shop, 15 Duke Street, Dublin 2 (Tel. 01-6605663) and online at
www.nelsonshomeopathy.com.

Liz Earle's Naturally Active Skincare SPF15, which I have used myself and really liked.

Weleda Sun Lotion SPF15 is also waterproof and available in health stores.

Origins Factor 20 sun cream.

After suns

Green People Cool After-sun
Liz Earle's Naturally Active Skincare Sun Shade Botanical After Sun Gel

Protecting your skin from the sun

Human skin was not meant to be roasted in the sun. It takes as little as 15 minutes for the sun's rays to harm your skin, even though it may take up to 12 hours for your skin to show that it is sunburned. Here are some general tips:

- Every time you go out, you should protect your skin.
- Avoid exposure to sun on any part of the body that has been treated with radiation.
- If you have had lymph gland removal, you should wear a long sleeve top while in the sun or protect that area with a high protection sun factor.
- Use products that have a proper SPF factor. The SPF factor will tell you how long you can stay in the sun without getting sunburned.
- Make sure that you tan gradually.
- Use waterproof or water-resistant products if you are going swimming. Remember to reapply if you don't feel you have enough protection after swimming.
- Stay in the shade from 11am to 3pm or if it is very hot.
- Wearing a hat is good protection.
- Sunglasses are a great protection for your eyes. It is important that all glasses have the CE mark, which shows that they conform to European standards.

LYMPHOEDEMA

Lymphoedema is the swelling of the limbs and body owing to the accumulation of lymph. Lymph fluid is a colourless fluid forming in the tissues of the body and normally draining back into the blood circulation through a network of vessels and nodes called the lymphatic system. Lymph nodes act as filter stations and play an important part in the body's defence against infection, by removing excess protein, dead or abnormal cells and bacteria.

The removal of any or all lymph nodes in a particular area can result in an accumulation of lymph fluid in the surrounding tissues, and swelling occurs. Stagnant lymph forms a solid component, making the control of swelling more difficult.

In the case of breast cancer, where some of or all the lymph nodes under the armpit (axilla) are removed, or where there has been radiation to the lymph node area, lymphoedema (oedema = swelling) can occur in the affected arm and surrounding body.

How to recognise Lymphoedema

Lymphoedema can occur at any stage post surgery/radio-therapy, and particular attention should be paid to the affected arm at all times in order to catch and treat it early. You should look out for the following signs:

- 👍 Swelling in the affected arm that does not improve significantly with elevation.
- 👍 A general ache or heaviness in the affected arm.
- 👍 Swelling that feels soft and spongy to touch.

How to treat Lymphoedema

Lymphoedema can be managed successfully, even though it can become chronic. Any sign of swelling should be attended to immediately by visiting your Consultant/GP. If you know of a Manual Lymphatic Drainage (MLD) therapist or a specialised Physiotherapist, it is a good idea to contact them to see what is required. Each case will be different. They will measure your two arms and determine the severity of your lymphoedema, treat accordingly and supply you with the correct-fitting sleeve. In order to contain the swelling, a compression sleeve is worn daily and removed when going to bed at night or while taking a bath/shower. The sleeve should be comfortable and snug and should cover all parts of the swollen arm. There are many different types of compressions available, ranging from elastic to custom made in a variety of compression classes. Compression mittens are also available for swollen hands/fingers.

As the sleeve is fitted, it can be difficult to put on. However, an 'easi-slide' – a plastic sleeve with a loop at the end – fits easily on the arm and the compression sleeve glides over it up the arm. Then place the loop at the end around a secure object such as a door handle and pull – the plastic sleeve will glide off the arm, leaving the compression sleeve in place.

For the more adventurous amongst you, an American company, Lymphedivas does a range of colourful sleeves. Check out their website *www.lymphedivas.com* for more information.

Manual lymphatic drainage

Manual lymphatic drainage can remove excess fluid from the arm. It works by opening lymph nodes in unaffected regions such as the neck area and then massaging the fluid towards these unaffected lymph nodes, thus helping to drain the affected area.

Manual lymph drainage is a gentle but much specialised form of massage, so it is very important to go to a qualified MLD therapist to receive it. A list of these therapists by area is available on the website *www.mldireland.com*. Click on Therapists, then on the appropriate area on the map, and a list of MLD therapists in that area will be displayed with their contact details.

Other forms of therapy, such as bandaging, are also available from MLD therapists, who, depending on the severity of your lymphoedema, will recommend the most appropriate treatment. Bandaging is the application of several layers of padding and short-stretch bandages to the affected arm. This encourages lymphatic flow and helps to soften fluid swollen areas.

Lymphoedema increases the risk of certain skin problems such as cellulitis. It is very important to keep the skin on the affected arm/area clean and moisturised. Cleansing with antibacterial washes and moisturising with tea-tree moisturiser/oil is recommended – tea-tree has antiseptic qualities and will help to minimise the risk of contacting infections. Just be aware that tea-tree oil can be too astringent for some dry skins. Lavender, coconut and almond oils are also effective for skin maintenance.

Deep breathing and daily exercises (supplied by your therapist) will help to promote lymphatic flow. You should always wear your sleeve when doing your exercises.

Treatment for lymphoedema can be costly and it is wise to check out the cost in advance of treatment, and whether or not your medical card/tax (MED 1 form) or medical insurance covers the treatment. At the time of writing, some cover is provided by Quinn Healthcare and VIVAS Health but no cover is provided by VHI.

How to help prevent lymphoedema
In order to help prevent against lymphoedema, care and attention should always be paid to the at-risk arm. If you have had any or all axillary (underarm) nodes removed, you should have a compression sleeve to wear when flying (even for short haul flights) as a preventative measure.

You should have been given a set of instructions and exercises in the hospital post surgery. It is very important that these instructions and exercises become part of your daily life because lymphoedema can occur at any time.

Some dos and don'ts that should be incorporated into your daily life:

Do's
- Do keep skin clean and moisturised
- Do avoid cuts, scrapes, bites and burns (be careful when ironing or cooking)
- Do treat cuts and other wounds as soon as possible – clean the skin well and apply an antiseptic solution or antibiotic ointment
- Do use a high factor sun screen
- Do use insect repellent
- Do use a thimble when sewing
- Do wear protective gloves when gardening or washing dishes/clothes
- If you travelling abroad, get a prescription for antibiotics or take them with you in the event of injury, bites or cuts to your affected arm. It would also be a good idea to take an antibiotic cream with you.

Don'ts
- Don't take unusually hot baths or showers
- Don't use hot-tubs, saunas or steam-baths
- Don't apply heat pads or hot compresses to the arm, neck or shoulder on the affected side
- Don't carry heavy objects
- Don't wear a watch or jewellery on the at risk arm/hand
- Don't permit injections, bloods to be drawn or blood pressure to be taken on the at risk arm.

PROSTHESIS

When breast cancer surgery results in having a full mastectomy, there can be a major change in how you look. You will feel differently about your body image. For some people, this change can be extremely difficult. It is a life-altering situation for any woman. No matter how strong the person is and how much support she has, every woman must deal with the loss of her breast in her own unique way and in her own time. I myself did not have a full mastectomy, so, even though I have come through breast cancer, I cannot fully appreciate how anyone feels who did.

Breast prostheses are breast forms that are placed inside a bra to make your breasts look natural and balanced. I have spoken to my friend Noreen, who has just had a mastectomy. The Breast Care nurse talked to her soon after her surgery about having a temporary breast form fitted. It is lightweight and will minimise irritation to the sensitive scar area. This can be worn following surgery, and it will make sure that your outward appearance is maintained after the operation. This was done in the hospital before she went home and she found the fitter very helpful. Six to eight weeks after the surgery, you can be fitted with a permanent silicone breast form. These are designed in such a way that they closely resemble a natural breast in terms of weight, appearance and texture. Following breast surgery, all women are entitled to their first prosthesis and two bras free of charge.

When you leave the hospital setting, you will then have to make you own arrangements to have fittings done in the future. Many of the Cancer Support Centres have a service where a fitter comes to the centre. This can be once a month; each centre has its own arrangements. There are also some specialist shops, that offer this service.

I met Mary, a fitter, in the hotel room she rents; the room was nice and comfortable and has a pleasant ambience. Having worked for years in the business, Mary has a lot of knowledge and experience. She told me that women are very nervous when they arrive but leave with fresh confidence and a feeling of femininity once they have helped and fitted properly. Mary also stressed that a client is always told that if she's not happy with what she has bought when she gets home, she must ring her. She was adamant that the client must be happy or otherwise she may feel rather despondent. It is very important that you are happy with what you have bought.

Here are some tips that should help. Wherever you go to get fitted, make sure that:

 It is private.

 It is warm and comfortable.

 There is adequate stock from which you can choose.

 There is a seat for you to sit down and a full-length mirror for you to view yourself in.

 The fitter should be sensitive to your needs.

 You should be informed how to take care of your prosthesis.

 You should be able to contact the fitter if you have any problems.

Am I not a Woman?

My shape has been changed.
My form has been revised.
My breast has been de-sized
Am I not a woman?

My heart still loves.
My arms still hug.
My body still craves.
Am I not a woman?

My hips still swerve.
My lips still entice.
My eyes still allure.
Am I not a woman?

My fingers still caress.
My mouth still soothes.
My ears still listen
Tenderly.

Am I not a woman? (*Author Unknown*)

Care of your Breast Prosthesis

It is important that you treat your Breast Prosthesis with reasonable care because they can split. They usually come with a two-year guarantee and therefore should be replaceable within that timeframe. In the event of your Breast Prosthesis splitting, don't panic, since they will usually retain their shape once in the bra.

Swimming and Prosthesis

Swimwear with a pocket for your Breast Prosthesis is also available from the suppliers listed below and you can be fitted for a swimsuit at the same time as your Breast Prosthesis and mastectomy bras.

If you are an avid swimmer, then you are advised to get a special prosthesis that will not get damaged by chlorine/salt water. Ask your fitter for more details. If you are just an occasional swimmer, then there is no harm in using your everyday prosthesis.

Changing your Breast Prosthesis

Unfortunately, your Breast Prosthesis does not grow or shrink with you, so you may have to go up or down a size. If you have private health insurance, remember to check with your health insurance provider to see if you are covered when this happens. If you do replace your Breast Prosthesis, keep the old one. For occasional swimmers, you can use the old one in your swimsuit, which saves you changing the Breast Prosthesis from your bra to your swimsuit and back again.

To find a fitter, call the Action Breast Cancer Freefone Helpline at 1800 30 90 40. They have a list of fitters for the whole country.

Breast Prostheses suppliers list (at time of writing)

CARLOW
Marie Sue Lingerie,
27A Fairgreen Shopping Centre, Carlow.
Tel. 059 91 39639
Email: mariesuelingerie@eircom.net
Website: *www.mariesuelingerie.ie*
Prostheses, mastectomy bras, swimwear and full fitting service available. Medical cards accepted.

CAVAN
Suzanne Michaels Lingerie
Farnham Medical Practice,
Farnham Road, near Cavan General Hospital, Cavan.
Tel. 047 81377 or Mobile: 087 798 0804
Email: monaghanbrafitter@yahoo.co.uk
Fitting service offered first Thursday of every month by appointment only. Prostheses and mastectomy bras. Medical cards accepted.

CLARE
Rockford's Pharmacy,
21 Parnell Street, Ennis, Co. Clare.
Tel.065 682 0099. Fax: 065 684 4650
Email: *rochford@eirpharm.net*
Prostheses, mastectomy bras, swimwear and full fitting service available. Fitting service by appointment only. Medical cards accepted.

CORK
Bellisima,
Rubicon 2, Westside Centre, Model Farm Road, Cork.
Tel. 021 420 9030

Email: bellisima@ireland.com
Website: *www.bellisima.ie*
Bras, prostheses and swimwear, all from various suppliers, in stock. Fittings carried out by nurses, by appointment only Monday-Friday. Medical cards accepted and private sales.

Versacchi,
6 South Ring Business park, Kinsale Rd., Cork.
Tel.021 4627400
Website: *www.breasts.ie*
Personalized private appointment consultations for all measurement and fitting of post surgery breast prosthesis and bra wear. Medical cards accepted.

La Femme, 80 Oliver Street, Cork.
Tel. 021 427 7956
Email: lafemmelingerie@eircom.net.
Women caring for women. A personalized private consultation service for all measurement and fitting of post surgery breast prosthesis and bra wear.

DONEGAL

McElhinneys, Main Street, Ballybofey, Co. Donegal.
Tel. 074 913 1217
Fax: 074 913 1757
Email: roisin@mcelhinneys.com
Mastectomy bras and swimwear in stock. Fitting service by appointment.

DUBLIN

Almacare Ltd.,
Unit 11 Kinsealy Business Park, Kinsealy Lane, Malahide, Co. Dublin. Tel. 01 542 0413

Fax: 01 443 0640
Email: almacare@iol.ie
Website: *www.almacare.ie*
Bras, prostheses and swimwear in stock. Fitting service by appointment. Clinic held in north and south Dublin as well as in Galway, Sligo, Drogheda and Navan.

Versacchi,

175 Kimmage Road Lower, Dublin 6W.
Tel. 01 490 0570
Website: *www.breasts.ie*
Personalized private appointment consultations for all measurement and fitting of post surgery breast prosthesis and bra wear. Medical cards accepted.

O' Hara's Pharmacy,

16 Redmond's Hill, Aungier Street, Dublin 2.
Tel. 01 479 3136
Fax: 01 478 9618
Email: oharamedical@msg.ie.
Prostheses, mastectomy bras and swimwear in stock. Fitting service available Monday-Friday, 9.30am-5.30pm by appointment only. Medical cards accepted.

Everywoman Fitting Suite at Murray's Medical,

20-21 Talbot St., Dublin 1.
Tel. 01 823 0613
Email: info@everywoman.ie
Website: *www.everywoman.ie*
Prostheses, mastectomy bras and swimwear in stock. Fitting service by appointment only. Monday and Wednesday 10.00am-3pm; Tuesday, Thursday and Friday, 9.00a -5pm. Medical cards accepted.

Arnotts,
Henry Street, Dublin 1.
Tel. 01 805 0400
A range of mastectomy bras available in stock.

Roches Breast Care Fitting Service,
153 Lower Kimmage Road, Dublin 6W.
Tel: 01 492 6829
Fax: 01 492 7857
Email: breastcare@roches.ie
Website: www.roches.ie
Choice of prostheses, breast forms, mastectomy bras, lingerie, swimwear and accessories. Fittings in discreet feminine space; Monday – Saturday preferably by appointment.

GALWAY
University Pharmacy,
University Halls, Newcastle Road, Galway.
Tel. 091 520 115
Prostheses, mastectomy bras and swimwear in stock. Fitting service by appointment only. Medical cards accepted.

Anthony Ryan's Lingerie Department,
16/18 Shop Street, Galway.
Tel. 091 567 061
Mastectomy bras and swimwear in stock.

Dr Zita Fitzpatrick,
The Post Mastectomy Care Clinic, Cloghscoltia, Barna, Co. Galway.
Monthly clinics also at the Out Patients Department at Roscommon Hospital (Tel. 0906 626 200);
Portiuncula Hospital, Ballinasloe.
(Tel. 0909 648 200); and

Tuam Cancer Care Centre, Tuam, Co. Galway.
(Tel. 093 28522).
Full fitting services for bras, prostheses and swimwear. All consultations are free and by appointment. (Evening and weekend appointments possible) Medical cards accepted.
To contact Dr Zita Fitzpatrick
Tel 086 262 4385 or 091 592515
Email: zita_fitzpatrick@hotmail.com

Tuam Cancer Care Support and Information Centre,
Dunmore Road, Tuam, Co. Galway.
Tel. 093 28522
Email: tccg@eircom.net
Website: *tuamcancercaregroup.ie*
This cancer support centre organises fitting days regularly. Please phone the centre for further information.

KILKENNY
WH. Good,
88 / 90 High Street, Kilkenny.
Tel. 056 772 2143
Bras, prostheses and swimwear in stock. Sew in pocket service also available. Medical cards accepted.

LAOIS

The Cuisle Centre,
Block Road, Portlaoise, Co. Laois.
Tel. 057 868 1492
Fax: 057 866 6515
Email: info@cuislecentre.com
and cuislecentre@eircom.net

LONGFORD

Cherche la femme,
14 Dublin Street, Longford.
Tel. 043 334 4004
Email: Sharonannedevlin@hotmail.com
Prostheses and mastectomy bras in stock. Full fitting service available.

LIMERICK

Bravelle,
1 The Glen, Ballyneaty, Limerick.
Tel. 061 351886 / Mobile: 087 9397899
Email: pauline@bravelleshop.com
Website: *www.bravelleshop.com*
A range of prostheses, mastectomy bras and swimwear in stock. Fitting service is available by appointment. Mail order service available. Medical card accepted.
This cancer support centre organises fitting days regularly, Please phone or email the centre for further information.

LOUTH

The Gary Kelly Cancer Support Centre,
George's Street, Drogheda, Co. Louth.
Tel. 041 980 5100
Fax: 041 980 5101
Email: info@gkcancersupport.com
Website: *www.gkcancersupport.com*
This cancer support centre organises fitting days regularly. Please phone or email for further information.

MAYO

La Belle Femme,
Chapel Lane, Claremorris, Co. Mayo.

Tel. 094 937 3652
Website: *labellefemme.ie*
Prostheses, mastectomy bras and swimwear in stock.
Pocketing service for bra also available. Fitting service is
available by appointment. Mail order service available.
Medical Cards accepted.

Cara Iorrais Cancer Support Centre,

2 Church Street, Belmullet, Co. Mayo.
Tel. 097 20590
Email: caraiorrais@gmail.com
*This cancer support centre organises fitting days. Please phone or
email for further information.*

Mayo Cancer Support Association,

Rock Rose House, 32 St Patrick's Avenue, Castlebar, Co.
Mayo.
Tel. 094 903 8407
Fax: 094 904 4877
Email:mayocancersupport@eircom.net
Website: *www.mayocancer.ie*
*This cancer support centre organises fitting days regularly, Please
phone or email for further information.*

MONAGHAN

Suzanne Michaels Lingerie,

51 Dublin Street, Monaghan.
Tel. 047 81377
Email: monaghanbrafitter@yahoo.co.uk
*Prostheses and mastectomy bras in stock. Fitting service by
appointment only. Medical cards accepted.*

SLIGO

Sligo Cancer Support Centre,
2A Wine Street, Sligo.
Tel. 071 917 0399
Email:scsc@eircom.net
Website: *sligocancersupportcentre.ie*
This cancer support centre organises fitting days regularly.
Please phone or email for further information.

TIPPERARY

Suir Haven Cancer Support Centre,
Clongour Road, Thurles, Co. Tipperary.
To arrange appointments for prosthesis fittings at Suir Haven,
please call Pauline on tel. 061 351886 or her mobile:
087 939 7899.

WATERFORD

Nursing Needs,
13 Gladstone Street, Waterford.
Tel. 051 874622
Prostheses, mastectomy bras and swimwear in stock.
Fitting service by appointment only. Medical cards accepted.

WESTMEATH

The LARCC Cancer Support Centre,
Ballinalack, Mullingar.
This cancer support centre organises fitting days regularly.
Please phone or email for further information.
Call Save 1850 719719 Monday to Friday
Tel: 044 937 1971
Fax: 044 937 1900
Email: info@larcc.ie

Silhouette Services at the Hope Cancer Support Centre,
22 Weafer Street, Enniscorthy, Co. Wexford.
Tel. 053 923 8555
Bras and prostheses in stock. Fittings by appointment only. Fitters
Catherine and Marie.

DRESS LIKE EVERY DAY MATTERS

Our clothes are too much a part of us for most of us ever to be
entirely indifferent to their condition: it is as though the fabric
were indeed a natural extension of the body, or even of the soul.
—QUENTIN BELL

WHEN I WAS GOING through my chemotherapy, I made a decision that I was not going to stay in my dressing gown all day. In my head, that was telling me I was sick and I rejected that notion. I felt it was a negative image. So every day during my chemotherapy I got up and got dressed. I decided to dress for myself and to look as good as I could. I decided that when I looked in the mirror I wanted to see a confident image reflected back, a positive outward appearance had a huge influence on my thoughts and mood. I put on make-up every day. It made me feel normal and part of the human race. I felt if I dressed well, I would feel better, and indeed, I did. There were days of course when I did not feel well and had to go for a rest.

My sister took time off work during my treatment. She would come to visit me every few days. She told me long after my treatment that she felt she had to get dressed up too because she knew I would have made a huge effort to look well. She was joking, of course, but she did say that because I looked well, it made those around me feel better too. There is definitely something in the phrase 'look good, feel good'.

Looking back on that time, it was probably my way of coping, but you know it worked. At that particular time, that was all that mattered. I loved to wear bright, happy colours. I bought a glamorous cerise pink coat and pink boots. I know the boots were a bit of a statement but they made me smile every time I wore them. They were my happy boots.

I believe now that there is no point in keeping clothes for a special occasion. Every day is a special occasion. When you are going through cancer or have come through cancer, each day is important. Keeping nice clothes hanging in your wardrobe is a waste of time. I would say wear them, enjoy them and step out in confidence.

Fiona, who went through cancer last year, talked to me about how she wished to look her best during her treatment. She would not always want to spend a lot of money on clothes, so she decided to go into Penneys with €20 and see what she would find. She said she had such fun buying brightly coloured socks, different coloured scarves and some jewellery and would come away feeling very happy with her purchases. It just gave her a lift on a day she might not have been feeling great.

Fiona had a mastectomy, which can limit what she wears, but she had a few great tips to offer. She'd had some pretty tops but these now needed a little adjustment, so she bought some thongs in Dunnes Stores or Penneys, cut out the lace and stitched it into the front of the top. Another option she found useful was to buy a wide headband (again at Dunnes Stores/Penneys) and sew it into the front of a low-cut dress.

And remember, there are a number of different ways to

source clothes during your treatment, including personal shoppers, on-line shopping, renting an outfit or shopping at department stores.

Personal Shoppers

I have explored some new ways of adding variety to your wardrobe at this time. For example, if you have a special occasion, such as a wedding, during your chemotherapy, you could treat yourself to a personal shopper to take you out shopping for an outfit. Very often people put on weight or lose weight during treatment and, as a result, they lose confidence in their appearance and in their ability to go shopping. If you are not well enough to go out shopping, a personal shopper will also bring clothes to you, having first come to your home to discuss your likes and dislikes with you. Wouldn't it be great if friends or family could give you a voucher for a personal shopper? It would be a special treat to go out to buy some nice clothes, once your treatment is all over. Many personal shoppers will also go through your wardrobe and help you sort out your clothes.

When researching personal shoppers for this book, I met some of them in person and spoke to all of them on the phone. Each had an understanding of people going though cancer treatment, whether through some of their own family members having cancer or assisting people undergoing treatment.

BELFAST

Ruth Cromie (Tel. 00 44 (0) 7834 986 207)
www.rpersonalshopper.com;
Email: style@rpersonalshopper.com

CORK

Rebecca Birchall (Tel. 087 987 4922)
Email: rebecca.birchall@gmail.com

Maeve Bancroft (Tel. 087 681 0189)
www.maevebancroft.com;
Email: maevebancroft@eircom.net

DUBLIN

Maureen Noone (Tel. 086 066 9066)
www.nothingtowear.ie; email maureen@nothingtowear.ie
You should check out Maureen's website as there are some very good tips on what type of clothes to wear after having different types of surgery.

Mary Holmes (Tel. 087 900 3494)
www.rubyseven.ie; email mary@rubyseven.ie

Antoinette Kane (Tel. 086 817 7317)
Email: antoinette.kane@gmail.com

Tara Crowley (Tel. 086 888 2838)
www.optomiseyourwardrobe.com;
Email: tara@optomiseyourwardrobe.com

Cathy McCrone (Tel. 087 295 9935)
www.imagestylematters.com;
Email: cathy@imagestylematters.com

DUNDALK

Caroline McElroy (Tel. 085 722 9975)
www.mya.ie; Email: info@mya.ie

GALWAY

Delilah Bouakkaz (Tel: 087-6391956)
www.delilahfashionstylist.com
email: delilahfashionstylist@gmail.com

LIMERICK
Caroline Cuddy (Tel. 087 836 5230)
www.stylebycaroline.ie; Email: info@stylebycaroline.ie

MAYO
Maggie Gibbons (Tel. 087 678 2406)
www.maggie-gibbons.blogspot.com;
Email: maggiegibbons@iol.ie

NATIONWIDE
Maria Kelly (Tel. 087 991 3236)
Email: info@mariakellyfashion.com

Dundrum Town Centre
The centre offers a styling service from Tuesday to Saturday, which you book at Tel. 01 299 1700. It costs €65 for two hours.

Free Service
Many of the large department stores including *Debenhams, Arnotts, House of Fraser* and *Clerys*, offer a personal shopping service.

Dress Hire
This is another option. Some people might prefer to hire a dress for a special occasion, since they may not wish to wear the dress again after their treatment. This is a very personal choice. *Covet – The Borrower's Boudoir* in the Powerscourt Centre, Dublin 2, offers this service. It stocks all designer labels, but they source only one of each piece, which they will alter to suit your size. They also have shoes and other accessories to match the outfits. The cost of hiring depends on the piece and the duration of time. The prices start at €50.

Covet, The Powerscourt Centre, 59 South William Street, Dublin 2, Tel. 01 679 9313 *www.covet.ie*; Email: info@covet.ie

Buying clothes on line

On-line shopping directory
Shopping on-line is relatively simple nowadays and the choice is vast. Whatever you decide to buy and regardless of where you source the merchandise, you can check the best price for any retail item on *www.kelkoo.co.uk.* This is a price comparison site that will help you find the very best price, no matter what you are purchasing.

For fashion and more

www.bunnyhug.co.uk
www.asos.com
www.smash-wear.co.uk (for a colour injection!)
www.very.co.uk
www.redrubyrouge.com (based in Holywood, Co. Down but you can also buy on-line)
www.belindarobertson.com (cashmere shawls and other bespoke items)
www.jigsaw-online.com
www.reissonline.com
www.hobbs.co.uk
www.rarefashion.co.uk (young cheap fashion)
www.oneboutique.co.uk
www.celtic-sheepskin.co.uk
www.doo-lally.com
www.madison-rose.co.uk
www.harrisonfashion.co.uk

Sportswear

www.earth-couture.com – organic designer (Kelly Hoppen)
www.fit2bseen.co.uk

Designer shopping on-line
Designer clothes are expensive, but there can be great value at sale times!
www.brownsfashions.com
www.net-a-porter.com
www.matchesfashion.com
www.mytheresa.com
www.my-wardrobe.com
www.collette.fr

For accessories
www.hamptonblue.co.uk (based in Northern Ireland)
www.etsy.com (US jewellery)
www.cherryrocks.co.uk (based in Northern Ireland)
www.cakejewellery.ie
www.farfetch.com
www.sunglasshut.co.uk
www.wantsunglasses.co.uk

For underwear and hosiery
www.mytights.com
www.roxburyandmcqueen.com
www.figleaves.com
www.maidenform.co.uk
www.vanillalingerie.com

Fragrance and candles
www.lelabofragrances.com
www.luckyscent.com

Plus size fashion
www.yoursclothing.co.uk
www.marisota.co.uk (size 12 − 32)

Footwear
www.rubbersole.co.uk
www.dune.co.uk

A MORE NATURAL BEAUTY

Not many people know or are aware of the numerous chemicals that are contained in so many of the beauty products that we use. Until very recently I was like most women and just bought cosmetics without thought; it is really only in the last year that I have become aware of websites, books and articles written on the many chemicals that are contained in a huge number of cosmetics. I also thought that if I bought a well-known, expensive brand I was guaranteed quality but that was, to say the least, naivety on my part. I was fooled into believing that expensive meant safe, but that is far from the case. In fact the expensive brands just have a lot more money to spend on marketing and advertising their products.

Since I have had my cancer, I am much more aware of the cosmetic industry and the many chemicals that are contained in so many widely used cosmetic products. I am now much more conscious of what I put on my body and have begun to re-evaluate the products I use. I quote from a book called *Toxic Beauty* by Dawn Mellowship.

'Mounting scientific evidence about the dubious nature of chemicals we are regularly exposed to in toiletries is encouraging a consumer shift in attitude towards the multi-billion-pound beauty industry. Organic and natural beauty brands are becoming more popular.'

But beware. You also have to be careful when choosing these products, because often they are not always what they seem. The term 'organic' is widely abused in the beauty world because, as yet, European law does not cover organic guidelines. Many of the Associations who use the

word 'organic' develop their own standards and there seems to be no general guidelines to which they all conform. Ecocert allows sodium lauryl sulphate (SLS) and parabens in products. The Soil Association has the highest standards for all health and beauty products. To be certified as organic by the Soil Association, the product must contain ninety-five per cent or more organic ingredients.

Information and knowledge is power, so try to become familiar with some of the chemicals in products. Do your own research on the contents of products, as there is an abundance of information available. The purpose of the following piece is to enlighten you to the many chemicals that are contained in everyday cosmetics. I was not aware of the numerous ingredients/components in products until I got cancer, and I list below some of those that you should avoid.

Parabens (methyl, ethyl, propyl and butyl, isobutyl)

Function   They are used as preservatives in foods, cosmetics and pharmaceuticals

Product   Types Moisturisers, shampoos, conditioners, hair shaving gels, nail creams, foundations, facial masks, skin creams, deodorants and baby lotions, toothpaste, hair colour/bleach, lipstick, lip gloss and eye shadow.

Health Concerns It can cause allergies and skin irritation.

Sodium Lauryl Sulphate

Function — Acts as a penetration enhancer by increasing the delivery of the active ingredients.

Product Types — Shampoo/conditioner, bar soap, body wash, face cleanser, liquid hand soap, acne treatment, hair dye, mascara, shaving products, toothpaste, sunscreen, make-up remover, perfume.

Health Concerns — This chemical alters the structure of the skin and allows chemicals to penetrate deep in the skin. It is a cause of eye irritation and can also cause contact dermatitis.

Petrolatum

Function — It is a petrochemical that forms a barrier on the skin, making lipstick shine, creams smoother and skin softer.

Product Types — Almost every personal care product, especially creams, lotions, wax depilatories, eyebrow pencils, eye shadow, liquid powder and lipstick.

Health Concerns — Petrolatum can cause allergic reactions. It is banned by the European Union.

Toluene

Function — It is used as a solvent that improves adhesion and gloss.

Product Types — Nail polish and hair dyes.

Health Concerns It affects the nervous system. It can cause fatigue, mental confusion, dizziness, nausea and headaches.

Formaldehyde

Function This chemical acts as a disinfectant, germicide, fungicide and preservative.

Product Types Deodorants, nail polish, soap, shampoo and shaving products.

Health Concerns It is considered a possible human carcinogen, may trigger asthma, irritates eyes and the upper respiratory tract, can damage DNA and is banned by the European Union.

Ethyl Acetate

Function A solvent, it dissolves or disperses other components.

Product Types Nail polish, mascara, tooth whitening, perfume.

HealthConcerns Eye and skin irritant. Avoid using it on your face.

Diazolidinyl Urea

Function This chemical releases formaldehyde and acts as a preservative.

Product Types Moisturiser, styling products, shampoo/conditioner, hair spray/dyes, anti-ageing treatment, facial cleanser, sunscreen, facial moisturiser, foundation, eye make-up, acne treatment, mascara, body wash/cleansers, deodorant, concealer, exfoliator powder, body scrubs, bath oils/salts, eye/contact care, lip make-up, shaving products, after-sun product, douche/personal cleanser, make-up remover, liquid hand soap, nail treatments, pain relief rub/ointment, and fragrance.

HealthConcerns   It may contain carcinogenic impurities and is associated with other significant health problems.

Tea, Mea, Dea

Function   These ammonia compounds are used as emulsifiers or foaming agents.

Product Types   Cosmetics.

HealthConcerns   They can cause allergic reactions, eye irritation and dryness of hair and skin. Any of the three can be toxic if absorbed in the body for a long period of time.

Hydroquinone (1,4-benzenediol, 4-hydroxyphenol, phydroxyphenol)

Function   Bleaching agent and antioxidant.

Product Type   Cosmetics, skin lightener, moisturiser hair colour/bleach, sunscreen, concealer.

Health Concerns   Skin and eye irritant.

Aluminium

This is a chemical salt with absorbent and disinfectant properties. It is very often used in deodorants and anti-perspirants and is easily absorbed into the skin.

1,4-Dioxane

This chemical by-product is not included on many ingredients lists. Produced by the ethoxylation process in cosmetics manufacturing, it is a known animal carcinogen and penetrates readily into the skin. When ethylene oxide is added to sulphates to soften them, 1,4-dioxane is born. More than 56 cosmetic ingredients are associated with this chemical. Look out for sodium myreth sulphate, PEG, oxynol, ceteareth, oleth and polyethylene.

Fragrance (Synthetic)

Fragrances may contain as many as 200 undeclared ingredients. There is often no way of knowing since companies do not have to reveal the chemical constituents of a fragrance. They can just list it as 'fragrance' when it may contain hundreds of chemicals. Potential problems can include headaches, coughing, skin rashes, vomiting, allergies and dizziness. Avoid the use of any product with the word 'fragrance' in the ingredient list, unless the label indicates that it is derived from essential oils.

Triclosan

Function   Preservative.

Product Type   Deodorant, deodorant sticks and gels, cosmetics, soap, mouthwash.

Health Concerns This may lead to allergic reactions or contact dermatitis.

Phthalates

Function   Solvent.

Product Type   Nail polish, hairspray, soap, shampoo.

Health Concerns Carcinogenic.

I am not trying to cause alarm but I would like to make you more aware of what you are putting on your body. You decide on how you will use this information. You do not have to throw out your entire make-up collection today, but maybe the next time you shop, you can be more mindful of what you are buying. Even the introduction of small, simple changes will make a difference and I am slowly trying to do this myself – it is not an all or nothing regime. You are spending money in any event, and you will discover that many of the products that are friendlier to your skin are the same price or very often cheaper than the products that contain chemicals.

Perhaps you might consider trying some of the following products that I have used and found to be more beneficial for my beauty regime?

Liz Earle

This is a range of beauty products that I have come across in the last year. They are no more expensive than many of the well-known brands, with prices starting at just €12. The Liz Earle range includes Cleanse and Polish Hot Cloth Cleanser, Naturally Active Skincare Superskin Concentrate and two varieties of Shower Gel. There are, of course, many other products but at the time of writing, they do not do any make-up products. These products are available only from Wild and Green, Milltown, Dublin (Tel. 01 268 3333) and the Liz Earle website, www.ie.lizearle.com

Dr Hauschka

These products have been around for a long time. The range includes cleansers, toners and moisturisers, as well as foundations, eye shadows, and others. I have used their foundation and I liked it. These products are also organic and are available from any good health shop.

Burt's Bees

These products are organic. They are available from any good health shop.

Origins

These are also organic products. They have counters in Dublin in The House of Fraser, at the Dundrum Shopping Centre; Clerys; Arnotts and The Boots Store in Liffey Valley Shopping Centre. They also have a counter in Debenhams in Cork.

Trilogy Products

This range of organic products are available in many health shops, as well as in Dublin's six Nourish Stores located at Wicklow Street, Donnybrook, Omni Shopping Centre, Liffey Street, the GPO Arcade and Nutgrove Shopping Centre.

MyChelle Products

This range of products is not yet well known but it is hoped that they will be available shortly in health stores and other shops around the country. I have used their skin repair moisturiser. The products can be purchased at Bee Emporium in the Blackrock Market, Co. Dublin which is open every Saturday and Sunday, and also online *www.MyChelle.ie*;
Email: info@MyChelle.ie Tel. 01 254 2590

EO Ireland

I came across this company recently. EO Ireland is the exclusive agent for EO products. EO stands for essential oils. They have no synthetic fragrance or dye, are paraben free, sodium lauryl sulphate-free and harsh chemical free. There is a range of shower gels, body lotions, hand soap and shampoo. You can contact Catherine Murphy at 087-678 8463. Email: *info@eoireland.com*. Catherine will offer a €2 discount per item and free Dublin delivery to people with cancer. Catherine can also post outside Dublin. The postage starts at €4.40. You can view all the products on *www.eoireland.com*.

Afterglow Cosmetics has a lipstick that is lead-free. It comes in a wide variety of shades. The company also has a mercury-free mascara, called Pure Soul Mascara. Check them out on *www.afterglowcosmetics.com*.

Tanning Lotions

Many tanning lotions contain dihydroxyacetone, which can cause allergies and contact dermatitis. I would suggest that you try one of the following:

Origins	The Great Pretender. I have used this one myself and liked it.
Green People	Self Tan Lotion
Lavera	Self-Tanning Lotion
Liz Earle	Naturally Active Skincare Sun Shade Botanical Self-Tan Spray

Tan Organics (made by an Irish Company)
Buy online at *www.skinlogiconline.com*. It is also available in pharmacies and in beauty salons, which are listed on their website under stockists. If you have a problem, phone 01 806 8600.

Toner

Atlantic Aromatics do a Rosewater toner. It costs about €7. It is available in any good health store. *Liz Earle* also does a toner. It is approximately €12. You can also use ordinary rosewater, which you can purchase in any pharmacy. I learned recently from a friend that you can buy a large bottle of rosewater in the Asian Market shops for €1.50.

Organic cleanser

Here are two nice tips:

- 👍 To remove make-up, use organic cold pressed olive oil or almond oil with a cotton cloth or cotton pad and warm water.
- 👍 Use jojoba oil or sweet almond oil as a moisturiser for dry skin.

Deodorants

To be perfectly honest, I never considered what was in a deodorant in the past. I just put it on in the morning, liked the smell and thought I was doing a great job. It was not until I had all the nodes in my arm removed because of breast cancer that I began to think about deodorants. It made me wonder what I was applying directly on my skin in this very sensitive area. Having done some research on deodorants, I realised that they contain aluminium. Dr Philippa Darbre of the University of Reading has this to say

> *I am not quite sure why anyone in their right mind would want to spray a 25 per cent solution of aluminium under their arms every day. It is absolute madness. People need to understand what is really in a pot of underarm cosmetics. It is just a toxic mess.*

Anyone going through radiation for breast cancer has to use a special crystal deodorant. These deodorants are available in good health shops. When you have finished your treatment, I would recommend the *Dr Hauschka* range. There are two different kinds, the herb-scented Fresh one, with sage and witch hazel, and Floral, scented with jasmine and lilac essential oils. They may be a bit more expensive than many of the usual ones you buy in the supermarket, but they are safer and last longer. You should think seriously about using an aluminium-free deodorant.

Perfumes

Recently I discovered that I cannot tolerate the scent of perfumes as I find the smell very strong and overpowering. Having since researched this I now know that perfumes contain many unknown ingredients. Product manufactures do not have to list all of their ingredients as they claim that they do not wish their competitors to know what is in their perfume mix.

It is difficult to source organic perfumes but during my research I have found the following which may be of interest to you. Pg organics, natural organic perfume – *www.pgorganic.co.uk.*
Burren Perfumery, which is an Irish Company with the Soil Association Certification and is worth a look.
www.burrenperfumery.com   www.aftelierperfumes.com

General make-up tips

- Don't share your make-up with anyone.
- Don't use make-up that is out of date.
- Don't use make-up that has a bad smell.
- Throw away any old mascara and buy a new one.
- Always remove mascara before going to bed. Mascara that is left on all night could cause eye problems.

Website Suggestions

Check out Paula Begoun's website, *www.beautypedia.com.* There is an abundance of information on make up, product recommendations, reviews and much more.

Two Irish Websites – worth a browse:

www.shopwithnature.ie (all natural products)

www.beautyfeatures.ie (includes a natural product section)

www.abbeynaturals.ie (handmade soaps made in Athlone)

AND SOME SPECIFICS...

Foundation

The secret is that less is more. Keep it natural. Buy a colour that matches your skin tone. Often during chemotherapy your skin colour can change. To apply the make-up, use small circular motions with a fibre optic brush, which you can buy in most department stores and chemists.

Concealer

Apply a pink tone underneath your eyes and on the lid. A yellow-toned concealer will cover up any redness in the skin. Apply powder to set.

Colour and Definition

For colour and definition you need to contour. Imagine where the sun hits your face, around the hair line, down the centre of your face and just underneath your cheek bone, and apply a face powder a few shades darker than your skin tone. Remember, only use this darker shade when contouring.

Blusher

Peach tones work well on fairer skin. Pink tones work well on sallow skin. When you are applying blusher, smile and apply to the apples of the cheek.

Eyes

Apply a matt base shadow all over the lid. Brown earthy tones work for everyone. Apply on the outer corner and blend in to the sockets – (C shape).

If you have no eyelashes ...

You can get definition by using an angle brush. Using a dark brown eye shadow, press it on with the brush. It is like joining up dots. Press on the eye shadow outside the lids, going from corner to corner. If you just apply the eye shadow in the middle of the lid, it makes your eyes look smaller. Use browns because they are soft and will blend in better. Even if you have blue eyes, brown tones are more of a contrast and will do a lot more to enhance the look.

Eyebrows

Use an angle brush to apply soft tones, such as grey or brown. Fill in the gaps to your natural shape. Use a grey or a light brown eye shadow to fill in the brows for a nice, soft, natural effect, rather than using a dark brown, which will not look as natural.

How to read a label

All personal care products on the market must list the ingredients on the label. Label reading can be confusing, so here are some tips to help you wade through the chemical names. You can approach ingredient lists in three stages.

Start at the end where preservatives are listed. Try to avoid:

- Words ending in 'paraben'
- DMDM hydantoin
- Imidsazolidinyl urea
- Methylchloroisothiazolinone

- Methylisothiazolinone
- Triclosan
- Triclocarban
- Triethanolamine (or "TEA")

Next, check the beginning of the ingredients list. Here you'll find the soap, surfactant, or lubricant that has been added to make the product work. Try to avoid ingredients that start with 'PEG' or have an '-eth' in the middle (e.g., sodium laureth sulphate).

Finally, read the middle ingredients. Here you'll look for some common – but not essential – additives that may bring excess hazard: fragrance and dyes. On the label look for 'FRAGRANCE,' 'FD&C', or 'D&C'.

FOOD & NUTRITION

The priority during the treatment of cancer is to follow general advice on healthy eating. This is particularly important during chemotherapy, because one of the major side-effects is that it takes its toll on the body, lowers the immune system and can affect the appetite. It kills the bad cells, but unfortunately it also kills good cells. In an effort to remain as healthy as possible during treatment, it is important to eat properly so as to build up the immune system. Eating well can help you to:

- Feel better
- Maintain your strength and energy
- Tolerate treatment-related side-effects
- Lower your risk of infection
- Heal and recover faster

Dietary Guidelines

Drink plenty of water because this helps to detoxify the body of harmful chemicals.

👍 Eat plenty of fruit and vegetables, such as onions, leeks, cabbage, garlic, Brussel sprouts, spinach, watermelon and tomatoes.

👍 Turmeric and ginger help to boost your immune system, so use both in cooking.

👍 Include grains, brown rice, nuts and seeds; for example, almonds, Brazil nuts, pumpkin seeds and sunflower seeds.

👍 Foods to be eaten in high amounts include broccoli, olives, sesame seeds, almonds and parsley.

👍 Eat fish three to five times a week; include mackerel, cod, sardines, tuna and salmon.

👍 Allow for variety in your diet so that you increase your chances of getting good nutrition.

👍 Limit your intake of refined and processed foods as well as foods with additives, colours, flavours and sugar-rich foods. Avoid foods that contain artificial sweeteners, such as saccharin.

👍 Reduce or avoid foods that are smoked, pickled or barbequed. Avoid deep-fried and greasy foods, which are difficult to digest. Use olive oil in your cooking.

👍 Avoid junk foods, soft drinks, salt and sugar. Use kelp, sea salt or a salt substitute.

Poor Appetite

You may experience loss of appetite, nausea or similar symptoms during treatment. Try to eat as well as you can. Here are some tips to help you:

👍 Eat your favourite foods at any time of the day. If you like breakfast foods, eat them at dinnertime.

👍 Eat small meals or have a snack every one to two hours.

👍 Avoid liquids with meals to prevent you from feeling full early. Drink your liquids between meals.

👍 Build-up drinks can be very beneficial for poor appetite. They are appetising and contain the nutrients you need. You will find some recipes at the end of the chapter.

👍 Keep high calorie, high protein snacks on hand, e.g. granola bars, nuts.

Tips to make food tastier

Cancer treatment may affect your sense of taste. I know from my own experience that I had a metallic taste in my mouth for many days after my treatment and, as a result, it was very difficult to eat. Everything tasted of metal. The taste will go away in time, but when you are living with it, it can be difficult.

General suggestions

- Food will taste better if it looks appetising.
- Keep yourself hydrated by drinking lots of fluids.
- Try ginger ale.
- Chewing hard sweets, mints or gum may help to alleviate a bad taste in your mouth.
- Try using plastic utensils when eating.
- If your mouth or throat is sore, avoid spices, acidic foods, hot foods or beverages, which may irritate it further.
- Maintain good oral hygiene.

When cooking, the following might enhance the taste and add flavour

- Barbecue sauce
- Teriyaki sauce
- Spices and herbs
- Wine vinegar
- Chopped onion or crushed garlic
- Ketchup
- Soy sauce
- Mustards
- Bacon bits
- Nuts

- On your cereal, use honey, sultanas, raisins, nuts or natural yoghurt. You could also try fresh fruit, such as bananas and strawberries.
- If you find sweet foods unappetising, you could opt for savoury snacks such as
  - Cottage cheese with chives and crackers
  - Crackers and cheese
  - Hummus
  - Nuts
  - Peanut butter
  - Savoury pancakes

Superfoods

There is much talk today about superfoods. Duke University Oncology Department states that while there is no dictionary definition of a superfood, the term refers to foods that are 'nutrient dense' for their serving size. A nutrient dense food provides substantial amounts of vitamins and minerals and relatively few calories. Examples are brightly coloured fruits and vegetables, whole grains, low fat and fat free milk, cheese and yogurt, lean meat, poultry, fish, eggs, beans and nuts. A list of superfoods includes:

- Fish
- Salmon
- Blueberries
- Avocados
- Meat
- Lemons/limes

- Mushrooms
- Spinach
- Broccoli
- Beans, kidney and lentils
- Sweet potatoes
- Nuts

Juicing for Health (courtesy of Nutritionist, Anna Collins)

When you don't feel like eating or have a digestive upset after treatment, juices can be a good way of getting nutrients. They contain essential nutrients to build energy and immunity. Although it is always best to eat the whole food since it contains plant fibres that promote healthy digestion, juices are the next best thing.

The juice recipes here use vegetables shown to contain disease-fighting agents. Dark green leafy vegetables, such as broccoli, watercress, cabbage and kale, are high in folic acid, which is needed for the liver to detoxify used drugs and help destroy stray cancer cells. Vegetables also contain potassium to maintain the body's correct acid/alkaline balance, which is disrupted in cancer. Vegetables are more health-giving than fruits because they usually contain less sugar. Root vegetables should be present in no more than one glass of juice a day because they are higher in sugars than other vegetables. See Anna's recipies on pages 112-13.

Which juicer?

Buy a large juicer if you can – small ones fill with pulp halfway through juicing.

Ideally go for a 'masticating juicer', which extracts more nutrients and can juice the most mineral-rich leafy vegetables. Masticating juicers extract juice at a lower speed and preserve more nutrients.

The Samson 6-in-1 is a good masticating juicer and judged a 'best-buy' by Which? magazine. At around €200 (2010 price), it juices leafy greens easily.

If you can't afford a masticating juicer, centrifugal

ones are widely available. They grate the vegetables and spin them very fast so the juice is forced through a metal mesh. The downside is that centrifugal juicers can't juice the healthiest green leafy vegetables and the heat they generate causes some nutrient loss in the juice, so it cannot be stored.

If you are juicing with a masticating juicer you could make enough juice for a couple of days. Add a couple of teaspoons of fresh lemon juice and store in the fridge in a glass jar/bottle filled up to the top and capped with a tightly fitting lid to avoid nutrient loss (air and light destroy some vitamins).

If friends are willing to help, get them juicing for you. If you are being treated using conventional chemotherapy, radiotherapy or antibody therapy, you need to enlist help before you begin treatment, because you may not have the energy once the treatment has started.

General Guidelines for Juicing

Use well-washed and scrubbed vegetables, organic whenever possible. If using non-organic produce, discard the outer leaves of leafy vegetables and peel all other fruit and vegetables since the peels contain the most chemical residues.

Commercial juices are pasteurised and stored for prolonged periods and therefore contain few vitamins.

Commercial vegetable juices, such as delicious V8 from good supermarkets, are still a rich source of potassium, even though they will be low in vitamins. While this juice is pasteurised (i.e. cooked), it still alkalises the body, which is particularly important for those recovering from cancer.

Aim to buy local produce. Shorter time between harvest and eating means more vitamins, e.g. the vitamin C in an orange decreases by 50% for each week after it is picked, so if your orange was picked six weeks ago in Israel, how much will be left?

The Organic Company and Bramble Hill sell good quality cloudy apple juice – handy for adding to fresh vegetable juice to liven up the taste. Cloudy apple juice contains more beneficial bioflavonoids than clear.

Biona blueberry or cranberry juice can also be added to homemade juices for extra interest and is pure. Cranberry juice drinks from the supermarket will be very high in sugar and low in cranberry juice, which is naturally bitter-tasting.

Juice made from concentrate may contain added sugar. Producers buy concentrate, which already contains sugar, and they aren't legally obliged to state sugar in the ingredients.

(All the following recipes make about 200 ml)

Green juices
When you juice green vegetables, you will probably want to have no more than 1/3 greens in the mix so it tastes good. It's more important to have a small amount of greens in your juice and drink it regularly than to use lots and never drink it again.

Broccoli burst
Broccoli is one of nature's superfoods. Carrots provide antioxidant vitamin A and sweetness in this juice.

> 1/2 cup fresh broccoli pieces
> 3 medium carrots
> 1 apple
> Small handful of fresh parsley
> 1/2 lemon, peeled (optional)

Try making other juice combinations, such as:
Kale, ginger and kiwi or apple
Carrot, watercress and lemon
Cucumber, tomato and apple
Carrot, apple and Biona Cranberry Juice
Strawberry, with added Biona Blueberry Juice

Health Tip

To enhance your immunity, add a knob of fresh ginger to the other ingredients when making any fresh juice. A piece the size of your thumb is a good amount to start off with when making a glass of juice. It has a warm taste and helps soothe an inflamed digestive system too!

Did you know?
Grapefruit contains a substance called neringenin, which slows down your liver's detoxification of drugs. If you are on chemotherapy or other medications, it is advisable to avoid drinking grapefruit juice since it can lead to toxic build-up.

In a book called *Cancer Survivor's Nutrition & Health Guide*, there are two key concepts that the authors Spiller and Bruce believe to be at the forefront of nutrition during and after cancer treatment, namely:

👍 The diet should be based on plant foods, with only limited amounts of selected animal products, such as low-fat or non-fat milk products.

👍 The plant foods should be as unrefined as possible, with all their natural goodness left undamaged.

Keeping these two concepts in mind, the writers were also of the opinion that the food had to be appealing and should taste good.

The Three Key Factors for Recovery, according to the Cancer Survivor's Nutrition and Health Guide *are:*

- Calories to supply essential energy. These are best obtained from foods with carbohydrate and foods with good fats. These foods include whole grains and cereals, peas, lentils, fruits, nuts and seeds, olive oil and wheat germ oil.
- Proteins to build and rebuild tissues in the body. These include non-fat or low-fat milk, yogurt, cottage cheese and ricotta cheese.
- Protective compounds to prevent the recurrence of cancer. These foods include fruits, vegetables, nuts and seeds.

Tips in a nutshell

👍 You need calories to give you energy. While you are undergoing treatment and after you finish all your treatment, eat the foods that will give you energy.

👍 People often eat too much fat, but the key is to have a low intake of animal fats and a moderate intake of fats from plant foods.

👍 The highest quality protein foods in the plant world include cooked dry beans, lentils, whole grains and nuts.

👍 A time when you are weak and do not feel like eating is the very time that you need to eat to build up your energy.

👍 It is not just the food we eat that we need to consider; we should also be looking at our lifestyle and do all we can to get well and to stay well.

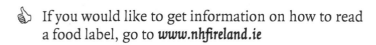 If you would like to get information on how to read a food label, go to *www.nhfireland.ie*

EXERCISE

To keep the body in good health is a duty...Otherwise we shall not be able to keep our mind strong and clear.

BUDDHA

At the outset I should say that I have always been a fan of exercise. By exercise, I do not mean working out in a gym once or twice a week. I mean walking. Before I was diagnosed with cancer, I took regular exercise and I know my good recovery after my surgery was largely attributable to my level of fitness. I was lucky, of course, to have had no complications of any kind during or after the surgery.

In 2010, I attended the Breast Cancer Conference in Dublin at which Marie Murphy was one of the speakers. A fitness and exercise specialist, she had just returned from the United States and had worked with Dr. Susan Love, an expert in the field of breast cancer.

At the time, the Irish Cancer Society was setting up a pilot study in a Physical Activity Programme for people who had come through breast cancer treatment. The programme involved fifty women volunteers to enable them to carry out the study. The conference provided the forum where women could volunteer to participate. There were two parts to the programme: walking and resistance training. The walking programme was open to anyone, but you had to be over your treatment for a year to partake in the resistance training programme. I attended the workshop given by Marie and decided to join the programme. In my opinion it is totally within the reach of everyone, even those who had never done exercise before. Depending on your level of fitness, it involved doing exercise three or four days a week, and any other exercise after that was a bonus. It did not matter how you got the exercise in, and it did not have to be completed all in one session. For example, if you were travelling home by bus from work or the shops, you could get off two stops ahead of your destination and walk the remainder of the journey. If that took ten or fifteen minutes, it could be included in your programme. The second part, the resistance training, consisted of attending a class once a week, learning how to do the resistance training, and then doing it also once a week on your own at home.

I will go through the two programmes individually.

Cardio-Vascular Programme

To commence the programme, you had to attend the Phoenix Park on a particular Saturday, where you walked a mile as fast as you could and your time was recorded by Marie to determine your baseline fitness measured in VO2/METs, which will be explained on page 114 of this chapter. This gave you a starting point and determined where you commenced on the programme. There were three Saturdays that you were obliged to meet in the Phoenix Park to be re-evaluated for your progress. This took place on the fifth, tenth and fifteenth weeks. You could join other walkers every Saturday, but only if you wished; otherwise, you could carry on with your programme at your own pace and time. The entire programme lasted fifteen weeks and the whole pilot exercise was recorded and evaluated.

Resistance Training Programme

You had to be a full year post surgery to commence the resistance training programme, which started in October 2010. I should emphasise that I had no previous knowledge or experience of weights. Marie evaluated me with ten exercises for the ten major muscles of the upper body. These exercises were done with one kilo weights to evaluate my range of motion in each exercise and to make sure my technique was correct to prevent any injuries. You can use two cans of soup or two water bottles to carry out these exercises at home if you do not have actual weights.

Once Marie was satisfied that I had full range of motion in all ten exercises and had established that I was fully capable of carrying them out, I commenced the training programme on the second workout. My very first work-out consisted of the ten exercises, each completed ten times, which resulted in my accumulation of 200kgs lifted in approximately 30 minutes. The programme lasted for twelve weeks, during which I increased the repetitions of each exercise or the number of sets in each exercise. Within four weeks, I had advanced to attaining a volume of 710kgs. My workout consisted of doing two sets of each exercise twelve times, lifting one and two kilo weights. By the eighth week I had advanced to lifting 1290kgs (two sets of each exercise fifteen times, using two and three kilo weights) and by the end of the programme, I had attained 1840kgs, doing two sets of each exercises twenty times, lifting three and four kilos. Just to clarify, the programme was using free weights, which means there are no machines involved; you are lifting the weights yourself which requires total balance and control while doing each exercise.

If you should like to know more about this programme, contact the Irish Cancer Society (tel. 01 231 0500). And if any group would like Marie Murphy to give a talk on nutrition or help them implement an exercise programme, you can reach her at tel. 085 196 5468, Email: coachmurphy@mbsfitness.com and
www.mbsfitness.com.

– Using Exercise to Reduce Your Risk of Developing Cancer or Experiencing a Cancer Recurrence

Recent studies have found that exercise reduces an individual's risk of developing cancer. Furthermore, in individuals who have already been diagnosed with the disease, exercise reduces the chance of a cancer recurrence as well as improves quality of life. But to reap all the benefits that exercise can provide, you need to be sure that your fitness routine is providing you with the right number of metabolic equivalents or METS. Studies have also shown accumulating at least nine METS a week reduces a women's risk of recurrence of breast cancer.

What are METS?

Exercise produces heat, which is why we get hot and sweaty while running, walking or doing other types of exercise. The amount of heat produced is directly proportional to the rate of energy expended and this is measured in METS. In addition, METS are a measurement of the body's capacity to utilise oxygen for a given workload.

No matter how much you weigh or how fit you are, you use 3.5 millilitres of oxygen per kilogram of body weight per minute to keep your vital organs working while you are sitting or lying down. This is written as 3.5 ml/kg/min, and it is equivalent to the rate of energy expenditure of one MET. In other words, 3.5 ml/kg/min = 1 MET.

Once you start moving, though, your fitness level has a direct impact on how many METS you expend per minute. For example, let's say you and your friend go for a three-mile walk. If your friend is able to process more oxygen than you in that distance, he/she can sustain higher METS and complete the three miles faster than you.

Know Your METS

If you don't know your METS, you won't know if you are getting the right level of exercise that is necessary to reduce your risk of cancer or a cancer recurrence. The first step to understanding METS is to calculate your weight in kilograms.

The next step is to figure out how many METS you are currently getting, and how many more METS you require to achieve your fitness goal. A total of 15-20 MET hours a week are needed to reduce your risk of cancer and other diseases. To achieve this goal, you should exercise for at least thirty minutes five days a week. Furthermore, while you are exercising, you will have to raise your metabolism 3-4 METS/hour.

So you and your friend get together with a group for a one-mile walk. Each of you accomplishes the goal, regardless of your fitness level. But the fittest individuals in the group will be able to walk that distance faster, which means they are acquiring more METS during the walk.

Say it took you 24 minutes to complete the mile. Walking at 24 minutes a mile is equivalent to raising your metabolism to 3.4 METS/hour (see table below). If you walk this pace five days a week for 30 minutes each day, you will accumulate a total of 8.5 MET/hours by the end of the week. (3.4 METS x 5 days a week = 17 METS/hrs/week. But since you are walking for only 30 minutes you need to divide 17 by 2, which gives you 8.5 METS/hrs/week).

Now let's say it took your friend 15 minutes to complete the distance. This is equivalent to raising your metabolism to 4.6 METS/hour. If your friend walks this pace five days a week for 30 minutes each day, he/she will accumulate a total of 11.5 METS/hour by the end of the week (4.6METS x 5 days a week = 23 METS/hr/week, divided by 2 = 11.5 METS/hrs/week).

To get enough exercise to reduce disease risk, you need to have 15-20 METS/hours a week. How can you and your friend get the added METS? There are three options – you could walk for an hour each day, instead of for 30 minutes; you could walk seven days a week instead of five or you could walk at a faster pace. To walk faster will require you to get fitter. But that's the pay-off. The fitter you are, the less time it will take you to achieve the required MET/hours you need.

On the two charts below, you will find additional information about METS. The first one is for a 30 minute walk, based on how long it takes you to go the mile, and how many days a week you exercise. The second one is based on METS acquired per hour.

Chart is based on 30 Minute Walking

Mins/Mile	METS/hr	3 days	4 days	5 days	6 days	7 days
40	2.6	4	5	6	8	9
30	3	5	6	7	9	10
24	3.4	5	7	8	10	12
20	3.8	6	7	9	11	13
17	4.2	6	8	10	12	14
15	4.6	7	9	11	14	16

Chart is based on METs per hour

Mins/Mile	miles/per/hr	METS/hr	2hrs./week	3hrs./week	4hrs./week	5hrs./week
30	2 mph	3	6	9	12	15
28	2.1 mph	3.1	6.2	9.3	12.4	15.5
26	2.3 mph	3.2	6.4	9.6	12.8	16

Mins/Mile	miles/per/hr	METS/hr	2hrs./week	3hrs./week	4hrs./week	5hrs./week
24	2.5 mph	3.4	6.8	10.2	13.6	17
22	2.7 mph	3.6	7.2	10.8	14.4	18
20	3 mph	3.8	7.6	11.4	15.2	19
18	3.3 mph	4	8	12	16	20
16	3.7 mph	4.4	8.8	13.2	17.6	22
14	4.3 mph	4.8	9.6	14.4	19.2	24
12	5 mph	5.2	10.4	15.6	20.8	26

Why do I like the exercise programme?

- 👍 I found Marie very encouraging. She loves what she does and was very happy to see people making the effort.
- 👍 She knows from research and experience how valuable exercise is in reducing your chances of your cancer reoccuring.
- 👍 I genuinely felt that this programme was within the reach of those people who had never exercised before. In fact, Marie was quite surprised that our group started the programme at a good level of fitness.
- 👍 I know that exercise helped me during my whole cancer journey. A programme that encourages any form of exercise should be recommended.
- 👍 Although I had never done weights before, I know now that they are very beneficial in helping to reduce the incidences of lymphoedema and other problems that are related to the after-effects of cancer.
- 👍 Marie illustrated that stretching and working with weights helps women who have undergone a mastectomy to rebuild muscle strength lost owing to surgery/treatment along with improving flexibility, range of motion and reducing the risk of lymphoedema.

In conclusion, I highly recommend this programme.

Why should you exercise during cancer treatment?

👍 It increases your energy levels.

👍 It helps stress, being beneficial to both your mind and your body.

👍 It can help offset weight gain.

👍 It can combat constipation.

👍 It can help you sleep better.

Walking, yoga and cycling are the forms of exercise that are particularly recommended during chemo but not swimming. That's because there is a drop in white blood cells during treatment, so people should avoid gyms, exercise classes and swimming pools because you could be putting yourself at risk of infection. Always check with your doctor or Health Care Team before you do any form of exercise.

Ten tips for starting an exercise programme after treatment

1. Get clearance from your doctor before starting any fitness programme.
2. Have a qualified Fitness Instructor guide/design your fitness programme.
3. Exercise a minimum of three days/week of cardio-vascular exercise (walk, swim, bike).
4. Exercise at least one day/week of resistance training (weights, Pilates, power yoga).
5. Set a goal of fifteen weeks to maintain consistency and see improvements in fitness.
6. Aim to achieve 15-20 MET/hrs/week within one year of training.

   Example: 5-10 METS/hrs/week 1-4 months
             10-15 METS/hrs/week 5-8 months
             15-20 METS/hrs/week 9-12 months

7. Ensure that your diet is healthy and nutritious – high in fruits, vegetables, whole grains and beans; low in fat and high in fibre.
8. Drink at least 1.5 litres of water a day (water is the most important nutrient).
9. Keep a record of your training to see how you improve; this will also help motivate you.
10. A little a lot is better than a lot a little. To do something often, you have to enjoy what it is you're doing.

Mummy, You Can Lift Me Again!

This is the story as told to me by J. Raftery, whom I met on the programme:

When I was first diagnosed with breast cancer at 35, I was devastated. Somehow I managed to put my own feelings on hold as the surgeon asked what I wanted to do next. The answer was automatic, as if I had it rehearsed – "Do whatever needs to be done to assure I will be around to see my two children grow up."

The weeks before my surgery I looked at my two children and wondered how I was going to lie beside them at night to read stories at bedtime or pick them up for a cuddle. I felt that cancer had rudely taken these simple things away from me without even asking.

After my surgery, I was determined to do my best to return to full mobility. Because of my surgery, I was unable to lift my daughter. I was very upset as I realised that children are only young for such a short time, and I felt I was being cheated. I then attended a talk by Marie Murphy (a Sports Consultant, Irish Olympian 1988) on 'How to reduce your chance of reoccurrence through exercise.' It was inspirational. I finally felt in control again. Marie began a pilot programme with breast cancer survivors through the

Irish Cancer Society. The twelve-week programme involved a cardio programme that included walking three to four times a week and a weights programme to strengthen upper body muscles. I had never lifted weights before in my life but it was amazing. Life began to return to normal with school runs, dinners and work.

One evening my daughter, who was just turning five, fell and began to cry. Without thinking twice, I scooped her up in my arms for a cuddle. She stopped crying immediately and looked at me in amazement, "Mummy, you can lift me again!"

That smile, similar to the one on Christmas morning, was one of the best things to happen for me in the previous year. I attribute this to the exercise programme and for the first time in months without thinking I was finally back to normal.

An illness like cancer can make you feel robbed of the precious moments you experience with children when they are young, but with the exercise and light resistance training that this programme offers, you can return to the person you were. This is priceless.

My children will probably always remember when their Mum was sick but I hope as they grow older they will remember the day that Mum was able to carry them once again.

This story highlights the value of the exercise programme and how its lasting effect goes way beyond what Marie Murphy had set out to do.

The Plurabelle Paddlers

The Plurabelle Paddlers are a breast cancer support group 'with a difference'. That difference is that the members – women who have been or are going through breast cancer – meet not on land but on the waters of the Grand

Canal Dock in Dublin, where they paddle in dragon boats, twenty abreast, in time to the beat of a drum.

The Plurabelle Paddlers are the first dragon boat team to be set up in Ireland. Fiona Tiernan, who has breast cancer, started the group in 2010. Determined to make her lifestyle healthier, she had been looking for new ways to stay active. She was frustrated that women like herself, recovering from surgery and chemotherapy, were not being encouraged to use exercise as a way to support recovery and a means to better long-term health.

Dragon-boating dates back to ancient China, and is surrounded by ceremony and myth. It is said that after exiled poet Qui Yuan threw himself into the water, distraught locals took to their boats in search of his body, beating drums to keep away evil spirits. The first modern dragon boat team was set up in 1996 by Dr Don McKenzie of the University of British Columbia. He was convinced that regular physical exercise would support women through treatment and recovery from breast cancer.

Dr McKenzie's team, Abreast in a Boat, showed that lymphoedema symptoms – common after breast cancer surgery – could be eased by repetitive upper-body exercise. Among the paddlers, no new cases of lymphoedema occurred, and none of the existing cases worsened. Women from all walks of life were brought together in a support group, which gave them a focus beyond cancer. The idea caught on, and there are now 150 teams worldwide.

Back in Dublin, Fiona persuaded oncology consultants Dr David Fennelly and Dr Jennifer Westrup to back the project, and in an amazing stroke of luck, signed up top UK coach Julie Doyle. Senior physiotherapist Ailish Daly also became involved and has given invaluable professional guidance for those women new to exercise, or returning to it with more limited arm movement.

The Plurabelle Paddlers have attracted interest from the outset. Significant financial backing from lead sponsors, the HSE and Breast Cancer Ireland, and other fundraising efforts helped purchase two brand new, fully kitted out dragon boats from Germany. An official launch at the Grand Canal Dock in October 2010 was attended by crowds of well-wishers. The women experienced for the first time the thrill of racing along the water, and the incredible force created by a team paddling in unison.

In winter, when the boats are in storage, the group meets twice monthly for exercise classes. Training focuses on improving flexibility and fitness, while strengthening the upper body. In warmer weather, the group paddles every week. So far, the membership is predominantly female, from a wide range of ages and fitness levels, but men are welcome. What brings everyone together is a desire to stay fit, but above all to have fun. The camaraderie has been incredibly positive and, in its own way, healing.

In the future, the Paddlers hope to attend other dragon-boating events worldwide and to host their own regatta in Dublin. Fiona sees the boats as providing excellent fundraising opportunities, and hopes to channel money towards research into lymphoedema, as well as Irish-led research on exercise and recovering from cancer. Longer term, she hopes to raise awareness of cancer through schools, with kids and mums competing in boats with and against each other.

NOTE: The Plurabelle Paddlers was set up by Fiona Tiernan and the above piece was written by Charlotte Coleman-Smith
To find out about the Plurabelle Paddlers...
Email: info@plurabellepaddlers.com;
www.plurabellepaddlers.com

A MIXED BAG OF PRACTICAL TIPS

👍 If you are not happy with a diagnosis, get a second opinion – It is your body and your life.

👍 When you visit your doctor/consultant, make sure to list out all your questions in advance. This time is valuable and you do not want to waste it. Take a friend if you wish, because, as they say, two heads are better than one.

👍 When you attend for chemotherapy, you could consider:
   • Bottle of water
   • Sandwich or snack that you would like to eat
   • Book, magazine or puzzle
   • Ipod or MP3 player
   • Wear comfortable clothes

👍 Accept any offers of a lift if you're going for a check- up or an appointment as parking can sometimes be a problem. There is nothing more stressful than having to worry about parking or having to find a meter. My sister drove me the first time I went in for my assessment and stayed with me. We were there for over three hours and she had to refill the meter while we were there. It was just so nice not to have to worry about it. If you do have to go on your own, make sure you have change for the meter, and also leave yourself plenty of time to get to your appointment. It does lessen the stress.

👍 If people offer to help you, let them. Not everyone wants to talk to you about your illness, but they may like to help in other ways, e.g. take you shopping, collect your prescriptions, mow your garden, do your ironing.

👍 The Bellarose Foundation is a charity that offers a home cleaning service free of charge to people with cancer. You can ring 085 843 5766 for further information. *www.bellarosefoundation.ie*

- Don't go to the dentist during chemotherapy. Either go before your chemo starts or wait until afterwards; this is to avoid getting an infection. Of course, if you have an emergency, you will have to go, in which case you should tell your dentist you are on chemotherapy.
- Drink plenty of water. I cannot emphasise this enough. Water is really a cleanser and flushes the toxins out of your body. Try to drink extra water the day before your chemotherapy because it helps to pump up your veins.
- Remember to pick up your forms for your bloods each time you finish your chemotherapy; you'll need them to have your bloods each time before your treatment.
- If you are having your chemotherapy during the winter, wear gloves or put a scarf over your hands on the morning of your treatment to keep your hands warm; this makes it easier for the nurse to find a vein. Soaking your hands in hot water is also very helpful.
- During chemo, if going out, I would wear gloves to help keep away infection. This is not so easy in the summer, but it very easy to do in the winter. I remember my daughter bought me a pair of teal blue gloves with little hearts on them. You could have matching colours for different outfits.
- Some people advise that you should wear a mask to reduce infection if you are travelling by plane during chemotherapy. If that seems very dramatic, a simple scarf over your mouth could also help.
- If you have troublesome body itch, calamine lotion is a soothing remedy.
- If you get dry eye, a side-effect I got during the chemo, gel tears are good. They can be bought over the counter at any pharmacy. You can also use vidisic gel for night-time, which is thicker and works on the eye during the night. You will have to get a prescription from your doctor for it.

- 👍 If you decide to have any treatments while on chemotherapy, e.g. beauty or alternatives such as acupuncture, it is very important that you let the practitioner/therapist know that you are on cancer treatment. Even if it is something as simple as getting a manicure, it is best to let them know.
- 👍 Wear sunglasses if your eyes are sensitive; they really do help. TK Max sells designer sunglasses at very reasonable prices.
- 👍 Choose a soft toothbrush when washing your teeth.
- 👍 If your mouth gets very dry, drink plenty of water. If you suck a sweet, that may also help. Avoid mouthwashes that contain alcohol because they can dry out your mouth.
- 👍 If you have a sore mouth, rinse your mouth with a solution of baking soda or salt and water. Use $1/4$ teaspoon of baking soda or $1/8$ teaspoon of salt in a cup of warm water. Avoid spicy or citrus foods, and sharp crunchy food. Eat food that is cool or at room temperature.
- 👍 When you finish a stage of treatment, celebrate it, whether it is your last chemotherapy session or your last radiotherapy treatment. Do something, buy yourself a gift. These are milestones and should be marked.
- 👍 Glucosamine supplements can help alleviate the joint pain that some people experience if on medication to prevent cancer reoccurrence. I take this twice daily and have found it to be effective. Ask your pharmacist or local health shop about the correct dosage and remember that it is advised to take it for at least six months to be effective, so don't give up. I also found tiger balm helpful. You can buy this in the health shop. You can also use Atlantic Aromatics oil for sports aches and pains and bruising. It contains arnica.
- 👍 If you have vaginal dryness, you can buy a product over the counter in the pharmacy called Replens.

👍 A friend tells me that she found a product called Lady Care to be very good for hot flushes. It's available in health stores for €25.

👍 If you have to take regular medication every day, buy a small pillbox and organise your tablets for the week. I find this very useful because I know if I have taken my medication each day. A friend of mine sets her phone to go off every day as a reminder to take her tablets.

👍 999 Medical ID & Personal Health Records Storage is a credit card with an integrated USB key which fits easily into your wallet. It stores all your personal medical records, allowing you to have them at hand at all times. The key plugs into any laptop or PC and you can immediately have access to details of your health conditions, allergies, treatment requirements, health insurance, medication or other specialist information. There are also stickers, which you can attach to your passport to identify that you are carrying this emergency card. It costs €34.99 and is available online on *www.999medicalid.com*

👍 If you have private health insurance, make sure you check out what is covered under your particular plan during cancer treatment. For example, if you have to buy a wig, you can claim a refund from your health insurance.

👍 If you go to the website *www.cincovidas.com*, you can print out a list of chemicals you should avoid and you can keep this in your wallet to check when you are shopping.

Aromatherapist, Fiona Hedigan has developed 'courage packs' for cancer patients. They consist of inhalers, which contain a blend of pure essential oils which help to relieve anxiety and nausea. Aroma Inhalers are being used in cancer hospitals in the UK – Christie's Hospital, Manchester and the Royal Marsden in London use them in their Complementary Therapy departments. Contact Fiona at *www.fionahedigan.com*

The majority of people who get breast cancer get the oestrogen receptor positive type. For some people there are nodes involved while others may have no node involvement. The Oncotype DX Test could be beneficial for those with no nodes involved. The major advantage of this test is that it will tell you if you need chemotherapy. If you have oestrogen receptor positive cancer with no nodes involved, talk to you doctor about this test. It is covered by AVIVA Health Insurance.

ACCEPTING HELP
Meals on Wheels

Your eating habits can change when going through chemotherapy. I remember before I had my surgery, I found it very difficult to eat. When I worry, I completely lose my appetite. It is important to try to eat good, nutritious food since you need it for energy and to keep your immune system sustained.

Before my cancer, I would always have cooked a few meals for a friend who had a death in the family or was going through a difficult time. Everyone has to eat and, as we all know, buying and preparing food takes time.

One of the most practical things I received when I was going through my chemotherapy was prepared dinners from friends and family. I found it very difficult to cook, particularly in the days following my chemotherapy. I sometimes felt weak and not really able to stand at a cooker and I didn't always feel hungry. If you have a family, that is not the case for them – they are not ill and still need to eat. So the meals on wheels were really welcome. I wouldn't always need to use the meals immediately, so I could put them in the freezer and nearly always had something to rely on when I was not able or did not wish to cook. My sister and sister-in-law prepared some appetising stews that were ideal for freezing. Friends also prepared great meals for us and quite often I just had to prepare some rice or potatoes. Such 'meals on wheels' are extremely helpful, particularly when you're going through the chemotherapy stage. But one small tip – don't forget to return the dishes to your friends, if only to get a refill!

Anyone who has read the book *Eat Pray Love* will know the passage where the author, Elizabeth Gilbert, compares her sister Catherine's world view with her own developing spiritual perspective:

"A family in my sister's neighborhood was recently stricken with a double tragedy, when both a young mother and her three-year-old son were diagnosed with cancer. When Catherine told me about this, I could only say, shocked, 'Dear God, that family needs grace.' She replied firmly, 'That family needs casseroles,' and then proceeded to organize the entire neighborhood into bringing that family dinner, in shifts, every single night, for an entire year. I do not know if my sister realizes that this is grace."

Another useful piece of advice was to prepare meals on the weeks that I felt well enough to cook. In my case, this was the second and third week after my chemo-therapy during which I would get my family to either do the shopping or to take me shopping. Then I would make casseroles and stews to store in the freezer.

You could also stock up on some prepared meals from Marks and Spencer or other supermarkets that stock them.

CARE TO DRIVE

Care to Drive is a service run by the Irish Cancer Society, which provides free transport for patients to and from their treatment. The volunteers, who are carefully selected and trained, collect the patients from their homes, deliver them to their appointments, collect them after these appointments and take them home.

The Irish Cancer Society, through a two-year partnership with Tesco for 2010 and 2011, is now able to roll out the Care to Drive programme nationwide. The background to the scheme goes back to 2006 when the Irish Cancer Society became aware that some families were experiencing great difficulty getting to and from treatment. The oncology social worker in St. Vincent's University Hospital approached the Society to endeavour to find a solution for patients who had transport problems attending the hospital. After talking to patients, identifying their needs and assessing if they would use a service if it were available, the Society adopted a model from the Canadian Cancer Society, calling it Care to Drive.

In 2008, the Society advertised for volunteers to be part of this scheme who would on a monthly basis take patients from their homes in south County Dublin, Wicklow and north County Wexford to St Vincent's University Hospital for their treatment. The volunteers had to attend a training programme.

A volunteer tells his story

John and his wife, Ann, have been volunteer drivers with the Care to Drive Scheme for approximately two years. They had a friend who died of cancer and when John retired he had time on his hands and wanted to do something worthwhile.

He did the training programme which he felt was very good preparation for the scheme. This operates only in St Vincent's University Hospital in Dublin at present although the Irish Cancer Society is trying to roll it out in the other hospitals. The wide catchment area for patients extends as far south as Gorey, Co. Wexford.

John told me that he had met the most amazing and

interesting people who were resilient, brave and grateful for the service. The day before the client's appointment, he rings to arrange a time for pick-up, gets the address and any other information, which means that the client feels reassured that he/she doesn't have to worry about getting to and from the hospital.

He is called on to help out approximately once a month but points out that there is no pressure to do a run if it isn't convenient; if he's going to be away, he will inform the Care to Drive organisers.

There are regular meetings between the Irish Cancer Society and the volunteer drivers. These have a two-fold purpose – the Irish Cancer Society can pass on information to the volunteers and the volunteers can discuss any issues that are of concern to them. It's a system that John feels works well and he's very happy to be a part of the team.

TRAVEL2CARE

The Travel2Care Scheme is a transportation assistance fund, which has been set up by the National Cancer Control Programme (NCCP) for patients who are travelling to the eight appointed Cancer Care Centres and is administered by the Irish Cancer Society.

In 2006, the National Cancer Strategy recommended that all major cancer treatment should be undertaken in eight designated specialist cancer centres, namely:

- Beaumont Hospital, Dublin
- Cork University Hospital
- Galway University Hospital
- Mater Hospital, Dublin
- Mid-Western Regional Hospital, Limerick
- St James's Hospital, Dublin
- St Vincent's University Hospital, Dublin

- Waterford Regional Hospital
- Approved Satellite Centre – Letterkenny General Hospital

The NCCP has identified breast cancer services as the first priority. At present, people diagnosed with breast cancer are entitled to claim financial help for travel costs related to their diagnosis and treatment.

The Travel2Care Scheme has now been extended to include the following:

- Patients with prostate cancer travelling to the Rapid Access Diagnostic Clinics in St James's Hospital, St Vincent's University Hospital and Galway University Hospital. The NCCP also plans to roll out the service in the remaining national centres of excellence.
- Patients with lung cancer who are travelling to the Rapid Access Diagnostic Clinics in operation in St James's Hospital, St Vincent's University Hospital, Beaumont Hospital and Waterford Regional Hospital. The NCCP also plans to roll out the service in the remaining national centres of excellence.
- Patients who are diagnosed with breast cancer through Breastcheck and receiving treatment in one of the eight designated centres or satellite centre.

The purpose of the Travel2Care scheme is to help with their travel costs those patients who genuinely find it a financial burden to get to and from their treatment in the designated cancer centres. It provides financial assistance if people are travelling by public transport, buses or trains; if they are travelling by private transport, it will help towards petrol and parking.

Information on the Travel2Care scheme is obtained

through the health care professionals in any one of the eight designated cancer care centres or approved satellite centre. Application forms can also be obtained from: Eimear Considine, Travel2Care, Irish Cancer Society, Tel: 01 231 6619 or Email: travel2care@irishcancer.ie

ACCOMMODATION AND TRANSPORT

If you are looking for accommodation in close proximity to your radiotherapy centres, the following may be helpful, not least because special deals are available.

Whitfield Clinic, Waterford

Ramada Hotel on the Cork Road offers deals to people attending Whitfield for radiotherapy. Phone tel. 051 336933 for further information.

Hermitage Medical Clinic, Dublin 20

There are also deals at the Clarion Hotel at Liffey Valley for those attending the Hermitage for radiotherapy. Phone tel. 01 625 8000

Beacon Hospital, Dublin 18

The Beacon Hotel offers deals to people attending for their treatment or you might consider renting an apartment on a short-term basis in Sandyford near the Beacon Hospital; there are also apartments in Leeson Street, Dublin 2.

Contact Patricia Mulligan for further information (tel. 01 639 1114 / Email: pmulligan@premgroup.com) or visit the websites for the Premier Suites in Leeson Street website at *www.premiersuitesdublin.com*) and for the Premier Apartments in Sandyford at *www.premierapartmentssandyford.com*.

Lancaster Lodge Hotel

Cork University Hospital has an arrangement with Lancaster Lodge Hotel on a B & B basis for people undergoing radiotherapy. It depends on the circumstances of each individual, type of cancer, how far they have to travel and other criteria. The nursing team decide on an individual basis who requires this accommodation and they make the arrangements with the hotel.

Cork University Hospital and the Mercy Hospital

Bru Columbanus, Wilton offers free accommodation to family members of seriously ill patients who need to have them close by. This applies to all the Cork hospitals, and the families are referred by the hospital. Families who live a long distance from the hospital are also considered. Contact Bru Columbanus at tel. 021 434 5754 / Email: brucolumbanus@eircom.net.

Inis Aoibhinn – Galway

Inis Aoibhinn is a house located on the grounds of Galway University Hospital. This wonderful facility was built through the fundraising of Cancer Care West and you can stay there if you are attending for radiotherapy in Galway University Hospital. Patients are booked by a referral made through the Radiotherapy Department at the hospital. It is a home from home facility and of great benefit to people who have to travel long distances for radiotherapy. The phone number is 091 545000; the Email: info@cancercarewest.ie.

Galway Clinic

If you are looking for accommodation close to the Galway Clinic, the Maldron Hotel (tel. 091-792244) offers accommodation for €65, room only (two people).

The Clare Galway Hotel (tel. 091 738300) offers accommodation for €69 room only (two people) and €80 room with breakfast (two people). Make sure you mention that you are going for radiotherapy when you are booking.

Accommodation benefit is something that may be covered by your health insurer, such as VHI, Aviva or Quinn Direct, so check with your health insurer to see if they will cover any of your accommodation costs.

Transport to Treatment

I came across two Cancer Support Centres that provide transport for people going to treatment. The Kerry Cancer Support Centre transports people living in Kerry to treatment in Cork University Hospital. The bus runs five days a week. It is a free service for people having treatment. It must be booked. You can ring 066 719 5560 between 9.00 and 1.00, Monday-Friday.

Arklow Cancer Support Centre transports people from the Arklow area to treatment in St Luke's Hospital, Dublin. The service is known to the social workers at the hospital and through the local GPs in Arklow. You can also contact the centre itself by emailing arklowcancersupport@gmail.com or ring 085 110 0066.

Sligo Transport

There is a bus that goes from Sligo General Hospital to University Hospital Galway every day, bringing people to radiotherapy. It will also accommodate people going for mammograms and other cancer appointments if they have space available. The bus is free for those who have a medical card and there is a minimum charge for non-medical card patients. The number to ring is 071-9177000 between 8.00-5.00 every day.

ENTITLEMENTS

The whole area of entitlements is a very complex one and not easy to navigate. If you have cancer, you may be entitled to certain payments but you have to apply for these, because they will not come to you automatically.

Tony Carlin, Principal Medical Social Worker at St. Luke's Hospital, Dublin was extremely kind and helpful to me. He kindly gave me permission to use the following information here. This chapter is his work.

A cancer illness is a very expensive time. The financial impact of cancer on a family is huge – 44% of people have said that cancer had made them less well off and 58% said that they had a decrease in their income. If people get a cancer diagnosis, they often have to dip into their savings to fund some of their bills. Transport costs can be a big factor in travelling to treatment. Paying for car parking can be prohibitively expensive.

Some helpful hints when filling out forms

- Write clearly in black pen.
- Make sure you have the relevant back-up letters from Social Worker, Doctor or Nurse to support your application.
- Make sure you always keep photocopies of any forms you send.
- Make sure you have the correct postal address to send forms to.
- If you get a name, always write it down.
- Always have your PPS number to hand.
- Check the form before you send it off.
- If you need help, ask someone to help you.
- If using the phone, give yourself plenty of time.

Medical Cards

- There is no consistency with regard to the allocation of medical cards.
- You have no automatic right to a card because you have cancer.
- They are means-assessed, based on income limits.
- If income comes solely from Social Welfare, you may be given a medical card, even if your income is in excess of the guidelines.
- You can appeal a decision if not granted a card – always do so; you have nothing to lose.

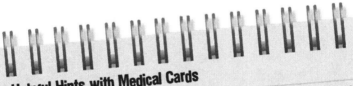

Helpful Hints with Medical Cards

- Make sure you fill in the correct application form MC1 and MC1a.
- Over 70s (MC1a) sent to Dublin – centrally processed.
- Under 70s (MC1) – local health centre.
- Always keep a copy of application form.
- Make sure to include the required documentary evidence to support your application; if you don't, the processing of your application will be delayed.
- Get a letter of support from your Consultant, GP, Social Worker, Counsellor – everything helps.
- If sending in application by post, register it.
- Hand-deliver if possible and get a receipt.
- Follow up your application with a phone call within the week to check that it has arrived.
- Get an approximate date as to when a decision on your application will be made.
- Always get the name of the person you are dealing with and keep a note of it.

Medical Expenses

If you have no medical card or no health insurance and you require hospital admission, you are required to pay €75 per night for a maximum of ten nights for one calendar year.

If you pay tax, you can claim back expenses for you and your dependants – MED1 Form.

Claim at the end of the tax year.

Enclose a P60 and receipts.

You can claim back a percentage of money paid for GP visits, nursing home fees, private carer's fee, the balance of any claim not paid by private insurance, on the first €100 paid for drugs while on the drug repayment scheme.

VAT can be claimed back immediately for any medical equipment purchased, e.g. stair lift, nebuliser.

Waiver of medical expenses. If you have no medical card and are finding it difficult to pay your medical expenses, you can apply to the relevant medical card section and request a waiver of medical expenses because of undue hardship.

You can apply for a medical card online, **www. medicalcard.ie** . You can also check the status of your application online.

You can download forms on line from **www.welfare.ie.**

If you worked previously in the UK or any other countries in the EU, you may be able to combine your social insurance contributions paid in Ireland with your social insurance contributions paid in another country. This can help you qualify for a social insurance payment in Ireland or in a country with which Ireland has a social welfare arrangement. You can do so by using an S1 application form (formerly E104). These forms can be downloaded from the internet or from:

Customer Operations

National Insurance Office
International Case Worker
Benton Park View
Newcastle-upon-Tyne NE98 122. UK
Tel. No. 0044 191 2037010

If you worked in Northern Ireland and are now resident in the Republic, you may be able to transfer some benefits and vice versa if you are moving to Northern Ireland.

You could check your entitlements with the Benefits Shop, Belfast. The phone no. is 048 903 36000. The Social Security number is 048 905 20520.

If you are disabled, you may be entitled to a number of benefits, such as disabled parking disc or tax relief on modifications to your car as a result of your disability. For further information you should contact the Disabled Drivers Association (tel. 094 936 4266) or the Irish Wheelchair Association (tel.045 893 094).

Financial Difficulties

If you have financial difficulties you should contact the Money Advice and Budgeting Service (MABS). This is a free and confidential service with offices throughout the country. The MABS helpline is 1890 283 438 (9am-8pm/ Monday-Friday) or email helpline@mabs.ie

Citizens Information Bureau

The Citizens Information Bureau is a very useful service for patients, offering advice on relevant issues, such as Disability Allowance, Illness Benefit, Invalidity Pension, Carer's Benefit, Carer's Allowance and Respite Care Grant. Information on any of these can be obtained from the citizens' information website at *www.citizensinformation.ie*

or from their freefone number 1890 777 121. You can drop in to any centre. You will get the listing in the Golden Pages.

If you worked abroad, you may be entitled to claim under contributions you made while working in another country. Check out the Citizens Information Booklet, under the section Combining Social Welfare Contributions from Abroad, Transferring Benefits from Abroad.

Financial Assistance

You can obtain some assistance from the Irish Cancer Society but this is given only when a person is in serious financial circumstances as a direct result of his/her cancer and when all avenues of assistance have been exhausted. If you would like to look for this financial help, contact your oncology or medical social worker at the hospital where you are being treated. He/she should then make the request in writing to the Irish Cancer Society.

Comfort Fund

The Marie Keating Foundation has operated the Comfort Fund since 2004. The Fund provides financial assistance to patients undergoing treatment for any form of cancer who find it difficult to meet their financial obligations. A cancer diagnosis can bring an additional financial burden to patients. Each year the Foundation allocates a specific budget through the Comfort Fund to help men and women, reviewing each case on its own merit. There is a ceiling on the amount given to each applicant.

You apply for this Fund through the breast care nurse or the oncology social worker in the hospital where you are attending, who in turn applies to the Foundation on your behalf. There are certain criteria to be met before you can apply for the fund. These are:

- Financial assistance will be considered for patients who are struggling financially as a direct result of their diagnosis during the treatment period; this includes palliative care.
- Either the breast care nurse or the oncology/senior social worker at the hospital, on the patient's behalf, must make all applications.
- It must be demonstrated that the patient is in immediate financial need and specific needs must be identified.
- Funds will be made available only to meet the patient's needs; the Comfort Fund cannot assist family members owing to the limited nature of its resources.
- One-time assistance will be only considered by the Foundation.
- Patients who have private medical cover or who are undergoing the application process for social welfare payments are not eligible to apply to the comfort fund.
- Patients who have already received financial support from other voluntary organisations cannot be considered by the Foundation.
- Payment will be made for travel/transport costs (this will not be paid to patients who meet the criteria for any other fund or scheme operated by statutory or voluntary agencies), childcare and household bills, such as increased heating and fuel bills.
- All requests should be made in writing and the situation surrounding the request should be explained, with an identified amount specified.
- A cheque will be made payable to the patient but issued to the breast care nurse/social worker who will then pass it on to the patient.

- Payment will not be made for medical or other costs that are covered by medical card, other state means or private healthcare plans.
- All applications will be processed within fourteen working days of each request.
- The Foundation requires written acknowledgement of the payment by the patient.

I have touched only briefly on the question of entitlements as The Irish Cancer Society has recently produced a book called *Social Welfare Support – A Guide for Cancer Patients*. It is comprehensive and can be obtained by ringing the National Cancer Helpline 1800 200 700.

The longer I live, the more I realise the impact of attitude on life.
Attitude to me is more important than facts.
It is more important than the past, than education, than money, than circumstances,
than failures, than successes, than what other people think or say or do.
It is more important than appearance, giftedness or skill.
It will make or break a company...a church...a home.
The remarkable thing is we have a choice every day
regarding the attitude we will embrace for that day.
We cannot change our past ... we cannot change the inevitable.
The only thing we can do is play on the one string we have, and that is our attitude ... .
I am convinced that life is 10% what happens to me and 90% how I react to it.
And so it is with you ... we are in charge of our attitudes.

(CHARLES. R. SWINDOLL)

PART 2

You Choose your Attitude

ROM THE FIRST MOMENT that I got my cancer diagnosis, I decided I was in charge of my attitude. I made a very conscious decision that I was going to beat my cancer. I remember bargaining with God, telling Him, 'Ok, I have been given this for a reason, but I am telling you now I am going to get through this and I am going to be well. This is a challenge I did not expect but I will take it on.'

Please do not misunderstand me. This positive attitude did not mean that I didn't sometimes feel afraid, uncourageous and vulnerable. There were times when I felt awful, both physically and emotionally, but overall I made a choice to be as good as I could be.

I met people along the way who annoyed me by their attitude. One person in particular comes to mind. During my radiotherapy treatment, there was a doctor who, in her own opinion, felt she was being realistic but in my opinion was totally negative. She did nothing to allay my fears of my impending treatment and when I met her a few days after starting my treatment, she never asked me how I was getting on. Instead, she proceeded to tell me all the things that were going to happen to me during the treatment. So, in turn, I told her that at that moment in time I was fine and would wait for all these things to happen but that I had no intention of pre-empting all this doom and gloom. I had come through major surgery, five months of chemotherapy and still had thirty-two sessions of radiotherapy to undergo and did not need to hear such negativity. If it arose, I would deal with it but in my head I had decided that I was not going to get any of the side-effects. For the record, I didn't get any of those side-effects that she talked about. I accept that some people might and they have to try to deal with them, but in my opinion it doesn't help anyone to list them all and say you will probably get them.

When someone tells you something like I was told, you have two choices – you either succumb to negativity or you rise above it and decide not to take on any unnecessary negative thoughts until you have some reason to do so. Always remember that you are unique and we are all individuals. It is the same with statistics. Some people just love to quote statistics and give you all those figures. You are not a statistic; you are a unique human being.

I was constantly trying to find ways to maintain a good attitude. For example, I had decided that after my lump was removed, my cancer would be gone. I remember that before my surgery, a part of me was dreading going in to hospital but another part of me could not wait to get it removed; I just wanted it out. I went to see my oncologist some time after my surgery to get a treatment plan for the chemotherapy. He gave me a great boost of confidence when he told me that my cancer was now gone, and the chemotherapy was purely preventative. I really believed what he said and it gave me courage and a very positive attitude for the next step of the journey. If you get good news, build on it, be grateful for it and move on.

> *Whenever problems seem to get the better of me,*
> *whenever I feel them closing in on me,*
> *I go to a quiet place that lies somewhere in my soul.*
> *I do not reason, analyse or think.*

Those will come later. I simply go.
From this place of silence, I garner strength and inspiration
to stand firm in the face of fire, to be calm in the midst of thunder.
When I emerge, the world has not changed, but I have.
And in changing, a whole new world is born.
(JOHN HARRICHARAN)

KEEP A DIARY

The act of putting pen to paper encourages pause for thought. This in turn makes us think more deeply about life, which helps us regain our equilibrium.

(NORBET PLATT)

I have always loved to keep a diary, and writing down events in my life, both happy and sad, has been therapeutic. It is very interesting to look back and read how you felt at a particular time. Writing is the key to the door, which unlocks the feelings that reside deep within us.

So when I got my cancer, it was no different. From the very beginning I kept a journal of events and how I progressed through the entire journey. I found it very beneficial to record happy times and sad times, and there was always a feeling of freedom to be able to express how I felt.

You do not need a wonderful command of the English language to do this. No one is going to read it except you. Even if someone were to, it is your story, your thoughts, your feelings at a particular time, and is not intended for critical analysis.

There are no rules here, so don't feel you have to write at a particular time each day – this is just for you. However, I suggest that you buy a journal or book that you like because you will be using it for a long time. I don't believe that a copybook is adequate; well, yes, of course it is, but it is better to have something that you like to use and that is special. There are various types of journals, notebooks and writing materials that you can buy at very reasonable prices.

I have spoken to a few people who have gone through cancer and they now regret that they did not keep a journal. Just remember, the entry does not have to be long, it can simply record the happenings of a particular day. You do not have to write every day; you may just choose to write on those particular days when something of interest occurs. There could be days when you won't want to write at all because you may feel too ill or too tired to be bothered. That is just fine, you do whatever suits you. Keeping a journal is a good way of handling the emotions that cancer triggers and helps people to clarify their thinking.

If you find a particular poem, quotation or piece that you like, keep it in your journal. My sister was in Greece during my chemotherapy and sent me a beautiful card of steps extending up to a beautiful pink sky and I put it into my journal. It was a majestic setting and made me believe that I could in time reach that pink sky. I just had to be patient, take one step at a time and I would get there.

I was looking back at my journal while doing my research for this book, and I was amazed at what I wrote.

The Irish Cancer Society has a very nice journal for people with breast cancer. The number to ring is 1800 30 90 40 and they will send it out to you.

There is also a new journal out now called "Keeping

Track of Your Cancer Treatment". If you would like a copy ring the National Cancer Helpline at 1800 200 700.

WHAT DO YOU TELL YOUR CHILDREN?

Begin with love and trust. It is very difficult to keep cancer a 'secret', particularly in a family. Even very young children can sense that something is wrong, and they may have questions, worries and fears. In the absence of accurate information, children might use their imaginations or misconceptions they may have heard to understand what is happening. Include them in explanations early in the family's experience with cancer.

(KAREN JANES, 2005 Talking with young children about cancer)

There is no better way to secure a child's trust than to be truthful with them always and particularly when times are difficult. They have a right to the truth and talking with them does help. Your child is more aware and clever than you think. Silence is not an option.

It is important that you tell your children about your illness as soon as you can. Children can sense rather quickly that there is something wrong if someone is ill, even if they are not told. We underestimate children and how they perceive things. If you have cancer and your children are at an age when they can understand, it is not good to keep them in the dark about mum or dad's illness. If they are not told they will be frightened and imagine that things are worse than they are. When I was about eight, my father was ill but my mother would not tell us what was wrong with him. I would fret and worry that he was going to die. I went through a dreadful time of anxiety. My mother thought she was doing the correct thing at the time, when in fact she was causing me far more stress.

The age of your children will determine how they are

told and what they are told. If you have very young children, a simple explanation is often all that's necessary. Young children don't dwell on anything for long and will take only in what is necessary at the time. If they ask questions, just give them simple answers. They do not require a huge amount of detail. You can reassure them that they can ask you questions at any time.

If you have older children, it will demand a lot more thought and consideration. They are more aware and, with technology so advanced now, they can easily Google information if they are computer literate. Let's face it; most young people have a vast knowledge of the Internet and websites today. My elder son, David was doing his finals at the time. I was so conscious of telling him the truth about my diagnosis, since he did not need the worry of his exams and, on top of that, dishonesty and misinformation on my part.

I would advise anyone with teenagers or older to monitor how they are feeling, and to ask them what are their needs, and listen to what they have to say. My own daughter told me about a year after I was finished my treatment that she would have loved to have spoken to a professional person/counsellor. At the time I was so absorbed in getting through the whole ordeal myself that I did not think to enquire if she needed help. In fact no one around me thought of it either. Not everyone wishes to discuss it with others, but there are some teenagers or young adults who would find it helpful to talk about their fears and anxieties. It was a lesson I learned. When my daughter asked me soon after I was diagnosed if she could tell her close friends, I told her she could, realising that she needed their support.

You should try to be as positive as you can when you tell your children about your illness. They may have heard that someone died from cancer, but remember that everyone's cancer diagnosis is completely different. There is a lot of research being done into cancer treatments and each year the doctors are coming up with new cures and many people survive cancer today.

If you have breast cancer and undergo chemotherapy, you will lose your hair. It is important that you tell your children this but also that it is only temporary and that it will grow back. If they are not told, they may get an awful shock when they see you with no hair. It is also important that they know you can get a wig or wear some nice scarves. They should know that there is no need for embarrassment when they have friends around to the house.

Janet Perioff was diagnosed with breast cancer in 2000 and became interested in the issue of communication with children about a parent's illness because she needed to explain her illness to her own son. Her concern for other parents with the same problem led to her developing a resource guide with Victoria M. Rizzo called "Conversations from the Heart: Resource for Talking to Children about a Parent's Serious Illness". It can be downloaded free of charge at *www.thelifeinstitute.org*

Things that help children
- Talking does help.
- Emphasise that your illness is not their fault.
- Give information in stages.
- Try to maintain a routine.
- It is important to let the school know.

I remember I told my children initially that I had to have surgery. I did not tell them until later about the chemotherapy and the radiotherapy. I felt that giving them the information in this way worked for me. I needed time to adjust to this myself and to get used to the idea of all the treatment I would have to undergo.

Things that won't help children
- Not telling your children you have cancer.
- Pretending that everything is ok.
- Trying to fix everything.

There are some good books on how to tell children that you have cancer. *My Mum's Got Cancer* by Dr. Lucy Blunt is a picture book that talks directly and openly to the child, with charming illustrations, which take away the secrecy of cancer treatment. The Irish Cancer Society has a book called *Talking to your Child about Cancer*. Other books include *No Matter What* by Debi Gilori; *Little Mouse's Big Book of Fears* by Emily Gravetts and *The Huge Bag of Worries* by Virginia Ironside. These books are used in the Climb Programme (see below). Books recommended by the Ulster Cancer Foundation include *The Secret C* by Julie Stokes and *Who will do my Hair?* by Rachel Smith and Joanne Robinson, who both work with the Ulster Cancer Foundation.

Whom do children talk to?
My research has shown that most Cancer Support Centres appear to talk to the adults, be it the person going through cancer or the older family members. So where do children go?

The Cancer Centre in Sligo has a wonderful programme of play therapy, art therapy and music therapy. Maureen, the co-founder of the Sligo Centre, had cancer herself and has huge knowledge and experience of cancer. Her passion and dedication for what she does is palpable.

Children often feel isolated; the Sligo Centre offers them a safe space where they can be themselves and express their fears. They also interact with other children in similar circumstances. They say a picture paints a thousand words and this is very true when it comes to children being able to express themselves through art and play. Children are not always able to put into words how they are feeling but when it comes to drawing and expression through play, they have the edge. It is a very valuable avenue for children to deal with emotion and trauma. Art therapy can help children express how they feel and, in turn, that can result in healing. The policy of the Centre ensures that only those who are properly qualified will be allowed to work with the children on such programmes because the Centre believes that what they explore in the various therapies will be with them for the rest of their lives.

The National Cancer Institute website states that when children of cancer survivors were asked what was important for them, they said:

- Being honest with them.
- Speaking as directly and openly as possible.
- Allowing them to become informed about your cancer and involved in your recovery.
- Spending extra time with them.

I have a friend who had breast cancer last year. Her only son went abroad for six weeks last summer and during that time she got the results of her tests, which confirmed her cancer. She had decided not to tell him until he got home but when she spoke to her consultant, he advised her that this was not the best approach and that it was important that she told him as soon as possible. She told her son over the phone in the most sensitive way she could. It subsequently transpired that Noreen had her surgery the day before his return so she was relieved that she had already spoken to him about her cancer.

Winston's Wish is a wonderful foundation whose website *www.winstonswish.org.uk* helps parents talk to their children when they have cancer and offers advice on how to help a child during a parent's illness. The website also assists children deal with bereavement of a parent through illness while recommending some good books that are worth a look.

Kidscope Inc. is an organisation which helps children and their families understand cancer and its effects on a family member. Their website is *www.Kidscope.org*

The Tuam Cancer Support Centre run a programme called Climb – Climb is an acronym for 'Children's lives include moments of bravery'. The programme is aimed at children between 5 and 12 years. It is a model, which is run by Rachel who works with the Ulster Cancer Foundation. It helps children to get an understanding of cancer and to dispel the myths and fears that surround the illness. Children realise that they are not alone and that other children are going through the same emotional upheaval. The groups use drama and art, have fun, and the children's interaction with other children is of huge benefit. If children are told the truth, in language that they can understand, when a parent is ill, they cope much better.

WE ALL NEED SUPPORT

> Dare to reach out your hand into the darkness, to pull another hand into the light. (NORMAN B. RICE)

My son Jack was 13 years old when I was diagnosed with my cancer back in 2007. Since then the mothers of three other boys from his class and the teacher in the primary school have been diagnosed with breast cancer. I was the first, then Mary, then Phil, followed by Emer and then Jack's teacher. There may be others. When Mary was diagnosed about a year after me and was going through her treatment, we would meet for a chat and a cup of coffee. One day she told me about Phil, who then joined us for the coffee, as did Emer, and now we meet regularly to support each other. We share any tips or information that we have gathered on the journey. I feel it is a great support. We are all walking the same journey.

It is a very informal group, but we know that we can depend on each other.

We meet every few weeks. Our conversations are not negative because we all wish to get on with our lives as best we can. We always have a laugh and Emer's husband has named the group the B Club. You can guess what B stands for.

Not everyone wants to talk about their cancer, and that's fine. But for those who do, you will meet other people during your stay in hospital for surgery, at chemotherapy and at radiotherapy. No one will understand what you are going through more than a person who is experiencing her own cancer journey. Noreen who is still having her treatment, has said to me that she realises now that she had absolutely no appreciation of what it was like for me at the time. She cannot believe how unaware she was and even questioned her availability to me during my treatment. I assured her that she did support me when I was ill.

You too can set up your own little group; you can meet informally or you could try to make it more organised.

How would you go about setting up a more formal group? Ann, a lady in Carlow, has told me how she and another lady set up a breast cancer support group by putting advertisements in the local paper, in the churches and any place where it would be seen by the general public. She also went round to all the GPs in the surrounding area to ask them to refer anyone who would like support from a group. It was a slow process, but they now have a solid group. They meet in a local hotel on the first Tuesday of each month. Sometimes they try to get a guest speaker for their meeting and they also go on outings during the year.

In Mayo, Louise, a cancer survivor, established a group for women in their forties who have cancer. Having had cancer herself, she wanted to do something to help others. The group is there to support those with any problems they encounter during their treatment. They do not sit around discussing cancer; instead, they do art therapy, set dancing and other activities, as well as going on outings twice a year. The women in the group come from all over County Mayo and the meetings are held at Rose House in Castlebar, home to the Mayo Cancer Centre, which allows them to use their facilities. Louise tells me that the women really enjoy coming.

My friend Fiona works with the disabled and her job entails trying to get people to reach out for help. When she got cancer herself, she realised she had to put into practice what she preached. She believed that it was very important for her that she looked for help and availed of the services that were there for people going through treatment. You meet people and it is good to talk. If you go inwards, it is not going to help with your recovery.

I read an article written by Tony Bates in The Irish Times Health Supplement (26 April 2011) based on the Dalai Lama's visit to Ireland. Within the article he affirms the positive long-term effects of seeking support during cancer treatment:-

"In his writings, the Dalai Lama has emphasised the intimate connection between our emotional lives and our physical wellbeing. He has often quoted David Spiegel's study at Stanford, which observed the benefits to patients suffering from severe cancer of sharing their experiences with one another on a deep emotional level. He arranged for one group of patients to meet weekly and talk about their cancer, while the other was required only to attend for regular individual check-ups. At the end of 10 years, it was found that those patients who belonged to the support group had twice the life expectancy of those who did not."

Reach to Recovery – Breast Cancer Support Group

Reach to Recovery is a Breast Cancer Support Group run by the Irish Cancer Society. Volunteers, who have themselves been through the journey of breast cancer, man it. Carefully selected and fully trained, they must be at least three years post treatment before joining the support group. There are over 50 volunteers spread around the country, all of whom must attend the annual refresher training courses.

Reach to Recovery volunteers provides one to one practical and emotional support and reassurance either by telephone or by face-to-face meetings. In order to ensure that you get the maximum support, you will be matched to the most suitable volunteer in terms of age, type of breast cancer, type of treatment, type of surgery, with/without children, age of children, location in Ireland and so on.

This support group gives you the opportunity to talk to someone who knows what you are going through, to discuss your fears and anxieties, share experiences, get practical tips and advice, and find out what to expect along your journey. The Reach to Recovery volunteer will provide as much support as you feel you need, be it one phone call or continuous support throughout.

Reach to Recovery is an internationally recognised Breast Cancer Support Group, active in most countries of the world, and was originally set up in the United States in 1952 by Terese Lasser, after her own operation for breast cancer. Reach to Recovery conferences are held in a different country each year and the international network aims to create closer links and encourage the sharing of information and experience between Reach to Recovery groups.

Reach to Recovery can be contacted via the Irish Cancer Society helpline, 1800 200 700. Further information is available on the website: *www.cancer.ie/action/recovery.php*. Volunteers also make hospital visits and are usually on hand for conversatins at Breast Clinics. Reach to Recovery literature is available in Oncology Day-Care centres.

Helping you through

Research has shown that when we face a major trauma in our lives, such as a cancer illness, friends and networks play a vital role in our recovery. It is often difficult to ask friends for help when we are in trouble. We frequently believe that we are a burden. But we don't have to ask one friend to do everything. Friends have different qualities and gifts. One friend may be a good listener, another friend may be much better at organising practical things, and another friend may be good at drafting questions before you visit your consultant.

In a US study, nurses who had been treated for breast cancer had four times less risk of dying during the subsequent years if they could count on the support of at least one or two friends. It was interesting to note that whether or not they had a husband had no impact on their survival. Only friends, usually female friends, made a difference.

YOUR CANCER SUPPORT CENTRE IS YOUR FRIEND

Asking for help is not a sign of weakness. No matter who we are or what we've been through, help is always available if we are open to receive. It is impossible to know the answers to all our problems. Be open to accept help and do not allow pride to be a stumbling block for growth.

(CHERI SCHULTZ)

To be perfectly honest, I never imagined I would need the services of a cancer support centre, but that's where I found myself on a cold winter's day in 2008. Lios Aoibhinn, the centre that I visited, has since closed down unfortunately.

I remember going in the door feeling fear, trepidation and mostly anger at having to be there and thinking that I wouldn't be if I didn't have cancer. It was, of course, so different from what I had visualised. The centre itself was bright, airy and very homely. The people working there were willing and eager to help you. They had a special understanding of what you were going through. They would tell you how wonderful you were to be coping (even if you did not believe you were!) and acknowledge what a difficult time it was for you at that point.

Now that I have experienced cancer, I believe that it helps to talk about it. A cancer diagnosis is traumatic and can be very stressful. Talking enables you to uncover shock, denial and anger. There is no easy way to bypass grief and pain. I believe that talking helps you *feel* the pain and loss and then you try to work through it. Unexpressed sorrow can lead to physical symptoms, including depression. It is so difficult to feel emotional pain, but it will serve you better in the long term. Suppressing how you feel is not a good strategy. Friends and family are of course a great support, but they are too close to you emotionally. A professional counsellor will listen to you in a non-judgemental way, because they are not connected to you in an emotional way.

> What I am saying is not simply the old Puritan truism that 'suffering teaches'. I do not believe that sheer suffering teaches. If suffering alone taught, all the world would be wise, since everyone suffers. To suffering must be added mourning, understanding, patience, love, openness, and the willingness to remain vulnerable. All these and other factors combined, if the circumstances are right, can teach and can lead to rebirth.
> ANN MORROW LINDBERGH, Hour of Lead: Sharing Sorrow

There are those who feel they could not visit such a centre. They may be in denial of their cancer, not want to talk or just don't believe that they need people at that time. I hope that this book will be of help to them and also show that dropping into a centre isn't such a daunting experience. A man at one of the courses I attended told me about a friend, a young woman, who would not consider going to a cancer centre. From talking to him, I felt she was a person who could have done with help, since she had never progressed after her treatment, was still full of fear and could not move forward in her life.

I attended a relaxation course at the centre and it was great to just forget about my treatment for a while. I also did courses in Stress Management and Mindfulness, where I met many interesting people, all of us trying to turn a bad situation into a positive one. We had coffee, we chatted and we laughed. We were a support to each other.

One of the women, a wonderful lady, has since died. She was such an amazingly positive person, so much so that I never knew that her cancer was as bad as it was until shortly before her death because she never complained.

Like most people, I came to use the cancer support centres when my treatment was completed. I found that it was later on, when I had time to really reflect on what I had been through, that I needed help. I went to the Beacon Cancer Centre for counselling. Suzy was wonderful, and with her help, the day arrived when I was able to tell her that I was ready to move on and that I was sure someone else might need her help more urgently. She agreed. It was a testament to both of us. I had done the work, but she had facilitated me in my recovery.

The centres offer treatments such as reflexology, massage and aromatherapy. It is a wonderful treat to go for a massage instead of a dose of chemotherapy. These treatments are free of charge. You can give a donation if you wish, but only if you can afford it.

All centres need a letter signed by your doctor that you can undergo any treatment.

SPECIAL PEOPLE WHO WALK THE JOURNEY WITH YOU

> I've heard it said
> That people come
> Into our lives
> For a reason
> Bringing something
> We must learn
> And we are led
> To those who help us most to grow
> If we let them.
>
> ('For Good' from Wicked, the Musical)

In the intricate web of the journey of cancer, you will meet many people – when you are in hospital having your surgery, when you are going through your chemotherapy and when you are undergoing your radiotherapy treatment. You become friends with some of them and obviously you will discuss the type of cancer you have and the various treatments that you are receiving. When you meet people through cancer, you have a lot in common. You will compare your cancers, your treatments and other information. You will meet people whom you believe have exactly the same type of cancer as you. Some time later you may learn that one of them has had a recurrence and you often go into panic mode. You think that it could happen to you.

When this happens, you have to be very careful not to compare yourself to that person. You may think you know all about your friend's cancer, but you actually don't. You do not know the person's history, what they were told by the doctors, what their prognosis was or if they had other complications, so you don't have all the facts. Every person and every story is different. You are your own individual. When you make comparisons, you become frightened and anxious.

This actually happened to me. I met Imelda, a beautiful person, when attending a Stress Management course in a Cancer Support Centre. Like me, she had breast cancer. While doing the course, she got a recurrence. I was shocked and upset for her. She had to undergo further chemotherapy. When the course ended, we kept in touch and would meet for coffee. Unfortunately she died about two years after her initial diagnosis.

When I spoke to her husband, he told me that her prognosis was poor from the very beginning. I didn't know this because she put up such a brave fight and was so positive right to the end. I never knew the full facts of Imelda's illness until she died. She was so strong and never let me know how difficult it was for her.

I believe that Imelda came into my life for a reason. She touched my life and I have lovely fond memories of her.

It can be extremely difficult when someone you met during your cancer journey dies. You can be extremely vulnerable and it can be a major setback to your recovery. It is especially difficult if it happens soon after you have completed all your treatment. But you have to keep focusing on moving on with your life and getting better. So please do not feel too despondent when this happens. I repeat: you do not have all the facts. Feel blessed that you are well and be thankful.

JUST LIVE THIS MOMENT

Life can be found in the present moment. The past is gone, the future is not yet here, and if we do not go back to ourselves in the present moment, we cannot be in touch with life.
(THICH NHAT HANH)

Many people with a cancer diagnosis look back on the past with regret or project themselves into the future. They do not grasp that they only have this moment, the present. All our regrets about the past won't change anything. All our worries about what might happen in the future won't add another minute to our lives and in fact may serve only to diminish our present moment. Even with cancer you have life, here and now. Many people put off doing things, waiting for the 'right time' to come, but if you always live with this mindset, life will pass you by. You have now, this day. Live it.

How many people say: if only I had not smoked, if only I had done more exercise, if only I had a healthier lifestyle … if only, if only. There is no point in looking back; it may only make you feel worse about yourself. People look to the future. What if the cancer comes back … what if, what if? Again you only have now, the present moment.

Regrets about the past will sap your energy and do nothing to enhance your life right now. Live for the moment and see how you can change things you may not have done in the past. One thing I learned is to take more risks. An old man, when asked what he would change if he had his life to live over again, said that he would take more risks. He would go outside his comfort zone and not be afraid to do things.

I attended a small workshop where Christy Moore was the host. He invited people to come up and sing with him if they so wished. I sat there thinking that I would just love to have the courage to sing with Christy Moore. I agonised over it before deciding that I might never get this chance again and so why not take it? I went up, sat beside Christy and we sang 'Nancy Spain'. I was shaking but the feeling afterwards was fantastic. I can honestly tell you that I wouldn't have done that before my cancer. I would have made every excuse not to do it. But now I don't really care what people think any more because they are too busy thinking about themselves to bother about me. So seize the moment and live that moment now.

I believe I have been given a second chance. I have a heightened sense of making the very best of my life. If opportunities now come my way, I take them. They may never come my way again.

Some ideas for living in the present moment

- 👍 Take notice of the world around you.
- 👍 Be mindful when you do things.
- 👍 Slow down.
- 👍 Be grateful for what you have.
- 👍 Be present for the moments that may seem insignificant. They may be the most memorable. 'Enjoy the little things, for one day you may look back and realise they were the big things.' (Robert Brault)
- 👍 Stop and breathe. Remember, your breath is the sound of life, a constant reminder to live in the moment.

Live life today. If you have your health today, say thank you and just enjoy today. There is no guarantee for anyone that they have tomorrow. Today is yours to live, today is yours to be, and today is yours to make a difference. Live it. At the end of your life, you don't want to look back and say, why did I not take more risks, why did I not live my life and have no regrets?

What will matter?

> What will matter is not what you bought but what
> You built, not what you got but what you gave
> What will matter is not your success but your
> Significance
> What will matter is not what you learned but what
> You taught
> What will matter is every act of integrity, compassion,
> Courage or sacrifice that enriched, empowered or
> Encouraged others to emulate your example
>
> (MICHEL JOSEPHSON)

AN ATTITUDE OF GRATITUDE

If the only prayer you ever say in your whole life is 'thank you', that would suffice.

(MEISTER ECKHART)

It is very easy to feel grateful when our lives are going well. In fact, when our lives are going along fine we are very often not even aware that we should be grateful. We don't stop to reflect on what we have and what we should be thankful for. But when you get a serious illness and your life is under threat, you have time to stop and think of all the things that you have taken for granted, the most important one being your health. The serious illness I am talking about here is cancer.

So why should you be grateful if your life is suddenly under threat? Perhaps because you may appreciate for the first time what you have been neglecting. When you are ill, gratitude is found in the most ordinary details of life. I believe that you are not going to be grateful for your big house or flash car, but instead will realise how blessed you are to have wonderful friends, family and people with whom to share important moments. You come to realise that the most valuable gift is not what you have in your life but who you have in your life. One friend I spoke to going through cancer told me she knew her friends were there but it was only when she became ill that she realised for the first time how strong their friendships were and how they stood by her.

I remember lying in bed on the days after my chemotherapy, not feeling very well, and getting text messages from friends. I may not have been able to reply, but in that moment I knew that they were thinking of me and I felt grateful for their thoughtfulness. I know, too, how wonderful it was to feel good. When the bad days passed, I had a heightened sense of wonder about life and living.

So how do you create an attitude of gratitude? Maybe each day think of just one thing you could be grateful for. It can be something really small. If you were to write down all these things, you would be amazed at how long the list would be.

Acknowledge moments of gratitude when you recall the people who have walked with you through your life – people who are now walking with you through your illness.

Awareness and gratitude stand side by side. To feel gratitude, you have to have your eyes open to see what you possess. Even in the midst of pain we can experience gratitude. Our pain is still there but is does not have to exclude a feeling of gratefulness.

If you need help, accept it and be grateful to have people who wish to help you. It is not a weakness to ask for help. We all need people whether we like it or not. To believe that you can always be self-sufficient is an illusion and sooner or later something will happen in your life that will shatter that illusion.

Life is full of surprises if only we are open to them. We often close our minds and do not see the wonders around us. E.E. Cummings says, 'The eyes of my eyes are opened'. What a beautiful thought. You are suddenly awake and alive.

Some thoughts on how to be a grateful person

 Treasure all that you have.

 Think about the positive things that have happened to you in the last week.

👍 Open your eyes to see the good things in your life, especially the small things. They are often the most important.

👍 I remember one day taking out all the greeting cards I had received from people when I was ill. They were so sincere and I felt a huge sense of gratitude, really blessed. In fact I did not realise I knew so many people.

👍 Be around positive people. It is difficult to be grateful if you are around people who are negative. These people bring you down and it is impossible to feel grateful.

👍 When I was ill, there were people thinking about me whom I didn't know. I had never met them and probably never will – they are friends of friends who genuinely wished me well. There was one girl in particular who works with my sister and apparently she always asked about me. Through a strange coincidence, I met this girl, and she was so genuinely happy that I looked so well and wished me all the best for the future. How could you not be grateful for all those wonderful human beings?

👍 I get up every day and I genuinely say thank you.

👍 I love to spend time in nature, because it grounds me and makes me realise what is important.

👍 I love to walk, particularly on a warm rainy day when I can feel the soft rain on my face.

👍 Each time I go for a check-up, I come out and just say thank you.

Maybe for the first time in my life, I truly value my health. I know this is difficult to understand, but because my life was under threat I believe I have been given a second chance. I have been given the opportunity to seriously re-evaluate my life and for that I am grateful. I no longer sweat the small things. Today I love my life, every day, every moment. I live those moments, because all we have are moments, the present moment. The following puts it into words so much better than I can.

You've never lived until you have almost died
For those who have had to fight for it
Life truly has a flavour
That the protected will never know.

(THEODORE ROOSEVELT)

THE SPIRITUAL PATH

Do not believe just because wise men say so.
Do not believe just because it has always been that way.
Do not believe just because others may believe so.
Examine and experience yourself.

THE BUDDHA (KALAMA SUTRA)

I believe to be truly happy you must search within and discover your own individual, authentic self. Actually, the longest journey is the journey inwards. But once you awaken your soul, and your search begins, there is no going back. Your soul is the inner face of your being. The essence of your soul is who you are and that is your light to the exterior world.

This journey has nothing to do with belonging to any particular religion. In fact that can often hijack your search. Life is a journey and there are many ways up the mountain, no one any better than the next. If you truly believe that a certain path is the right one for you, follow it. Don't let anyone tell you that you are wrong. It may be wrong for them, but perfectly correct for you. No one has a monopoly on the truth.

Religions often pull us away from who we truly are. They more often than not like to tell us what to do. Use your gift of wisdom and discernment to choose.

There are many ways to see the world. Certainly, if you could pick all the good bits from all the different religions, we could possibly have the secret to the perfect way to live.

I know I was brought to believe in a certain faith. I was told that the religion that I was born into was the one true way. I now cringe at the arrogance of any religious institution promoting such a belief. How could I have been so lucky? I know now of course that anyone with a different set of beliefs to me is just as correct in following his or her path. As children, we follow the path of our parents but as we get older and have our own life experiences we have a responsibility to think for ourselves.

There is a beautiful piece by Kahlil Gibran in the book *The Prophet* where he describes how parents cannot walk their children's path:

> Your children are not your children
> They come through you but not from you,
> And though they are with you, yet they belong not to you.
> You may give them your love but not your thoughts,
> For they have their own thoughts.
> You may house their bodies but not their souls,
> For their souls dwell in the house of to-morrow, which you cannot visit, not even in your dreams.
> You may strive to be like them, but seek not to make them like you.

This is a sobering thought for me having children of my own. I have to be careful that I allow them to follow their own destiny. I cannot live their lives for them. I have to allow them to make their own mistakes. I have to let go and give them space, choice and freedom. The more you try to cling to something, the more it just slips away. Let it go and it will eventually come back to you.

I have always been a searcher, a seeker, and a person to question. I have always pondered on the meaning of life, why certain things happen? I love to search, to wonder, to question and to seek truth.

Be patient towards all that is unsolved in your heart and try to love the questions themselves. Do not seek the answers, which cannot be given you because you would not be able to live them. Live the questions now, and perhaps even without knowing it, you will live along some distant day into your answers.

(RAINER MARIA RILKE)

There are many more questions than answers. When you begin the journey of questioning, you realise that there are no simple answers. People who tell you they have all the answers are not telling you the truth. They are afraid – they want certitude. They have not been tested. Anyone who has struggled has questioned. It is a human thing to ask, why me?

I believe that it is always our spiritual separation that causes our intense sense of struggle, in good times and in bad. Without touching the spiritual part of which we are, peace is absent, or at best fleeting.

(SUSAN JEFFERS, End the Struggle and Dance with Life)

We all have a spiritual side, although we may not wish to admit it or to call it that. Socrates states that the unexamined life is not worth living. It can take a lifetime to discover who we are. In fact it is not the destination that counts; it is the steps along the journey. Our many struggles, experiences and happy and sad moments all tap into our inner being.

The essence of spirituality is the search to know our

true selves – who am I, why am I here, what is my purpose in life? Spirituality has nothing to do with the ego – it is so much more; it is the search for the true self. When we discover our inner self, we find peace. We do not crave for material goods or recognition from others; we are free. It could take a lifetime to find this peace; we get glimpses of it from time to time. I like the definition 'religion is for those who don't want to go to hell, spirituality is for those that have been through hell'. I think that spirituality is a respect for all things and a tolerance of other people's opinions and goes far deeper than religion. It gives you a sense of being grounded, of a belief that there is something more, something greater than yourself. The Dalai Lama said, 'My religion is simple: my religion is kindness.' When Gandhi was asked if he would ever convert to Christianity, his answer was 'If I ever met one [a Christian], I would have become one.' What he was saying was, show me, don't tell me. My late friend Father Jack McArdle would always say that religion is caught, not taught. It is what you do and how you make someone feel that leaves the impression more than what you say. Believe in what is right for you and respect other people's ideologies in return. I know that spirituality comes from deep within your soul. It embraces all of you. It is not just for a Sunday; it is for every day.

If you get a serious illness like cancer, most of us ask the question, why me? But I asked, why not me? No one gets through life plain sailing. You may look at people and believe that they have the perfect lives. But how do you know that? You should never envy anyone, because you do not know his or her story, or what is deep in his or her heart. You do not know what they have to carry. It may all seem fine on the surface, but it is what is happening on the inside that counts.

You will never grow if you sit in a beautiful flower garden, but you will grow if you are sick, if you are in pain, if you experience losses, and if you do not put your head in the sand, but take the pain as a gift to you with a very, very specific purpose.

(ELIZABETH LESSER, Broken Open)

A question that Bernie Siegel poses in his book, *Love, Medicine and Miracles* is a question that many of you, including myself, could feel very aggrieved by. It asks: 'Why did you need the illness? He believes that this question helps the patient understand the psychological need that the disease may meet'.

Initially the question made me angry and very defensive. He was telling me that I caused my own illness. But when I looked at it more closely and examined it, I decided I should give it consideration and see if I could come up with some answers. The year before my illness, I went through quite a trauma in my personal life. It was a very stressful time. Had this anything to do with my getting cancer? I don't really know. Maybe I will never know. I reflect again on the quote by Rilke that there are more questions than answers. As human beings we feel we need to work everything out. It is all head stuff. Sometimes we may have to accept that life is a mystery and we may never have all the answers. As Rilke says, we may not be able to cope if we had all the answers. In a strange way, I believe that the personal struggle helped me when I discovered I had cancer. I realised from that experience that I was much stronger than I had given myself credit for.

I know how important my spirituality was to me going through my illness. It definitely gave me a sense of grounding, a sense of 'I will get through this'. I got a present of the book *Benedictus* by John O'Donohue from my friend Helena. It was the book I needed at that time. There was a piece in the book about how your life can change literally in seconds. When you get a cancer diagnosis, your life does change in seconds. When the doctor tells you, yes you have cancer; it is a life-changing event. I also remember reading in the book that the darkness I was going through had purpose, but that there was light, if only I could find it. I had to try and seek it. It is your thinking that darkens your world and if you can find that ray of light, it will help you. I love the song by REM, 'Everybody Hurts'. It is true, everybody hurts; we may all feel like giving up sometimes, but you have to hang in there. I realised how short life is and it made me think that I could make a difference as I moved on with my life. I truly believe that we can all make a difference in some small way and that we can leave a mark.

How can you make a difference?

Every day you should ask yourself, 'What one thing could I do today that would make a positive difference in my life and the lives of those around me?' You may ask yourself, what can I do? I am not famous, I am not rich, I am not powerful, I am just an ordinary citizen; so how can I make a difference?

The first thing you have to do is to change your attitude about yourself, because until you believe that you are special, you won't be. You have to believe that you can make a difference.

The great tragedy is that so many people go to their graves with their lives unlived, never having reached their potential. They were so busy living their lives by what was expected of them, or by trying to please others that they forgot to live their lives according to what they believed and what they desired.

It is a fact that there are people who love and care about you, but until you learn to love yourself, to believe in yourself, to know that you are unique, you will never truly be able to appreciate and love others.

You have the power to choose your attitude. You have the power to make a difference. Choose to make a difference. You have the power to create a vision of hope, to be a light for yourself and for all those around you. If you want to change the world, let it start with you.

> *Be the change you want to see in the world.*
> (MAHATMA GANDHI)

MEDITATION

My friend Maeve Garvey, a Meditation Facilitator and Counsellor, contributed this following piece on Meditation. It links her cancer experience with the benefits of meditation.

BE	STILL	AND	KNOW	THAT	I	AM	GOD
BE	STILL	AND	KNOW	THAT	I	AM	
BE	STILL	AND	KNOW				
BE	STILL						
BE							

'I was diagnosed with Inflammatory Breast Cancer in June 2003. Like everyone else in similar circumstances my world was blown apart on the initial receipt of this grim diagnosis. However, with the benefit of wisdom garnered through my psychological studies and previous life journey, I knew that in order to tackle my diagnosis and, indeed, survive it, I would have to employ a variety of tools/skills to get me back to full health and to guarantee my future wellbeing. I needed to reframe both my approach and response to my cancer challenge.

'I had always been reading books about Mount Everest and the incredible adventurers who pit themselves against this great mountain. I knew instinctively that Cancer was going to be my very own Everest expedition! My wonderful husband, children, family, friends and my cancer care team at St. Vincent's Hospital, Dublin became essential and wise expedition team mates! I need to acknowledge sincerely the wonderful care and support that I received from all of them throughout and without which I would not be here to tell my story today.

'I underwent chemotherapy, surgery, and radiation to hit my cancer hard with the big guns. While mainstream medicine played a major role in my recovery I feel I have to share that within my survival kit bag I had one very important item without which I could not have survived the expedition. It became my main source of oxygen supply and life support when times were particularly challenging. What was this essential piece of kit? MEDITATION.

'Over the years, prior to my cancer diagnosis, I was fortunate to have developed a keen interest in meditation and its various forms and practices. I had studied and partici-pated in a variety of techniques and learnt that Meditation can have numerous health benefits for the individual. Learning to develop my own personal practice was not always easy and required perseverance and trust. Thankfully, over time I learnt how to calm my busy 'doing' self and learnt how to achieve great inner peace which has had huge benefits in my life and helped me to cope with whatever life chose to throw my way. I learnt that Meditation could become a whole way of approach-ing one's life with considerable healing benefits for all. When you establish a den of peace within your core you feel empowered to act rather than react in distressing situations. A situation that seems hopeless when viewed from a perspective coloured with fear may become easily manageable when approached with a serene heart and peaceful mind.

'Many of the illnesses we experience over the course of our lives can be indicative of the body's attempts to process intellectual and emotional energy. When our body, mind and spirit are in balance, we experience good health. When we feel ill or we feel imbalance in our body, treating your whole self rather than treating the physical self alone can empower you to determine the root cause of sickness. Establishing a regular meditation practice can go a long way to assisting us in this process.

'There are numerous books, audio programmes and helpful websites to assist you in developing a meditation practice. Personally speaking, I found having a personal mentor/meditation teacher was of great benefit. I am also a member of a wonderful meditation group that meets weekly and is a powerful source of healing and personal development. Under *Resources* below, I list some of the books/websites/mentors that I have found useful.'

What is Meditation?

When the space between your thoughts becomes greater than the thoughts between the space.

(ALAN COHEN)

Meditation is often described as a training of mental attention that awakens us beyond the conditioned mind and habitual thinking, and reveals the nature of reality. Peace is possible and that is the intention behind any form of meditation practice, whatever the belief system that informs it. Meditation is like an anchor that keeps the storms of life from blowing you off course. While

Meditation can be hard work in the first instance, and indeed, this is the experience for many, with practice and perseverance one can learn to react less to their thoughts and to go on to enjoy the sense of spaciousness that a meditation practice will deliver.

There is a meditation instruction that compares the mind to a strong bull. It will go crazy if you lock it into a small paddock. But if you turn it out into a big pasture, it naturally quietens down. The big pasture is an attitude of mindful curiosity and spaciousness. In meditation we treat all thoughts – peace/sorrow, boredom/frustration, pleasant /unpleasant as equal. Thoughts are neither good or bad, they just are. Thoughts can be compared to clouds floating in a spacious sky. And that is what we are trying to develop: an attitude of spaciousness or big pasture within.

Meditation is a way of perceiving and being part of the flow in life. Through practice we develop a sense of spaciousness in the world. As we progress we become less prone to grab on to a stray thought that pulls us out of the spacious peaceful present. This spreads out into all our daily activities and our lives become a meditation shifting out of the ego's limitations (small-mindedness) and living instead in the infinite love and creativity of the Higher Self/True Essence/Presence/All that is/Spaciousness.

Approach meditation with an open heart. There is no perfect way or practice; different approaches will suit different individuals. Remember that to learn any new skill will require patience, practice and perseverance. It all begins with simply reclaiming your attention, so the first step is to bring yourself back into the present moment. Nearly all techniques share a common focus on the breath, how the body feels, or on a word or sound that is repeated silently or aloud. Be quietly aware of your own breathing and the feeling of your feet on the floor. Notice the sounds in the room and the tension in your shoulders. See that even as life goes on all around you, it is going on within you as well. Be aware that not only do you have a body, but that you are in it! This connects us to our true nature, our inner self. We are connected to what is real within us.

> If you would foster a calm spirit, first regulate your breathing; for when that is under control, the heart will be at peace; but when breathing is spasmodic, then it will be troubled. Therefore, before attempting anything, first regulate your breathing on which your temper will be softened, your spirit calmed.
>
> (KARIBA EKKEN, 17th-Century Sufi)

Diaphragmatic Breathing

Strong emotions tend to disrupt our breathing and trigger more shallow breathing patterns. By consciously shifting to diaphragmatic breathing, you can reduce the intensity of your emotional response and approach the situation more effectively.

The Relaxation Response

Some years ago I was very lucky to attend a seminar given by Dr. Herbert Benson, MD, a world-renowned Harvard Cardiologist. He spoke of the many physiological benefits of meditation in what he calls the 'relaxation response'. All forms of meditation in which the mind becomes quiet and focused elicit this innate response, which is the opposite of the body's stress or fight/flight response. He and his research colleagues found that it was possible for you, by simply changing the content of your thoughts (that is by thinking in a fashion called meditation), to significantly decrease your bodily metabolism, heart rate, rate of breathing, blood pressure, with consequent immune system benefits. Dr Benson describes the 'relaxation response' as a 'wakeful hypo-metabolic state' that is deeply restorative. It can quieten the rational mind, allowing a deeper wisdom to emerge. *The Wellness Book*, co-authored by Dr Benson, combines the best of what you can do to enhance your health and well-being with the marvels of scientific health care. It is the result of more than 25 years of scientific research and clinical practice at the Harvard Medical School and three of its teaching hospitals. It is a project of the Mind/Body Medical Institute and is a wonderful book if you want to learn more about mind/body interactions and how to use them to improve your health and sense of well-being.

Meditation is not an evasion. It is a serene encounter with reality.
(THICH NHAT HANH, *The Miracle of Mindfulness*)

Mini Relaxation Meditation

For a fast mini relaxation any time during the day, try the following:

- Take a deep breath and release it slowly – this is called a 'letting go breath'.
- Try breathing back from 10 to 1, one number on each out breath. By the time you get to one, you will notice that your breath is much slower and more regular and that you are relaxing.

Conclusion

If you want to connect with your own inner source of wisdom, power and peace, consider that what you are seeking is only a meditation away!

I wish you courage in your own journey and may you achieve true Inner Peace, which believe me can be as fantastic as reaching the summit of any great mountain!!

MAEVE F. GARVEY, *Meditation Facilitator/Counsellor*

RESOURCES
Books

The Wellness Book by Herbert Benson, MD; Eileen M. Stuart RNCM

And the staff of the Mind/Body Medical Institute of New England Deaconess Hospital and Harvard Medical School. A comprehensive guide to maintaining health and treating stress-related illness.

Timeless Healing –The power and biology of Belief by Herbert Benson MD

In this book Dr Benson shows how belief – especially belief in a higher power – makes a critical contribution to our physical health and offers a powerful, life-transforming blueprint for living.

Minding the Body, Mending the Mind by Joan Borysenko, PhD

A practical, straightforward book to help one gain control over racing thoughts and 'awfulizing'.

Full Catastrophe Living
by Jon Kabat-Zinn
The Relaxation and Stress Reduction Program of the University of Massachusetts Medical Centre.

The Miracle of Mindfulness
by Thich Nhat Hanh
A beautiful book in which Buddhist monk and Nobel Peace Prize nominee shares his wisdom in how to acquire the skills of mindfulness, a powerful Meditation technique.

The Complete Idiot's Guide to Meditation
by Joan Budilovsky and Eve Adams
An excellent resource and guide book to Meditation, full of helpful information, humour and wisdom.

Healing Psyche
by Rob Van Overbruggan, PhD
A treasure trove of rigorous research on the mind/body connection for cancer. He uses his expert knowledge of neurolinguistics and hypnotherapy to help clients use their minds to influence the cancer process.

Websites
www.healingpsyche.com
www.joanborysenko.com
www.alancohen.com
www.mgh.harvard.edu/bhi

Benson/Henry Institute for Body/Mind Medicine. (This site contains an online store with many relevant Meditation/Relaxation Response DVDs and CDs).

Ireland

Oscailt Integrative Health and Therapy Centre, Dublin 4
Tel. 01-660 3872
Beginner Meditation Classes (six-week courses) Contact Maeve at mfmgarvey@eircom.net

HAPPINESS

Being happy doesn't mean that everything is perfect. It means that you have decided to look beyond the imperfections.

(AUTHOR UNKNOWN)

I was lying in bed one morning thinking about happiness and trying to put into words what it is. These are some of my thoughts. I can tell you what it is not. It is not, as the media and advertisements would claim, to be found in wearing designer clothes, expensive perfume (probably full of chemicals) or trying to emulate the latest model. In fact, all these will serve only to make you unhappy, if the truth were told. It cannot be bought and that's why we are so disappointed if we think the contrary, leaving us empty and deflated. I have also realised that no material possessions can make you happy; they may bring you momentary happiness, but it will not last.

While people can share in our happiness, they cannot will us to be a happy person – that only comes from within. When I began to consider those who gave me some small insight into the meaning of happiness, two people came to mind immediately, two people who in some way capture a feeling of happiness for me.

The first is a priest friend, a monk but not a religious fanatic. He has a wonderful presence, a beautiful peace, a serene face and an intoxicating laugh; when you leave him, you are a better person for having been in his company. It is difficult to define but he makes you feel good about yourself and the world.

The second is a wonderful woman, Jane McKenna, who, in spite of losing both her children and facing every mother's nightmare, has such dignity and presence. She could be so unhappy with the world and bitter with people but she is the exact opposite. Anyone who has met her has been deeply inspired by her courage, presence and fortitude. While not wealthy in the material sense, she has wealth way beyond money.

I have read that you won't always remember what a person said, how they looked or the circumstance in which you met them. What you will remember is how they made you feel.

I believe that happiness is an attitude. It is a certain way of looking at life. There are those whose company you long for because they are positive, funny and full of life. In fact, they give you life. They have a way of looking at the world that is invigorating. Happiness is definitely an attitude and not just a set of circumstances. It is seeing the glass half-full. It is trying to garner the best in any situation. It is being happy in your own skin. It is not comparing yourself to others; it is valuing your own uniqueness. It is a state that we all desire, that is not easy to attain and that is the most difficult to define.

You don't always know you have been happy and it is only when you lose that happiness that you realise that you have glimpsed it. Patrick Kavanagh describes moments in life as 'glimpses through the hedge'. That is it. It may sound like a cliché but it is only when you lose that special thing that you realise how valuable it is. And so, when you lose your health, your perspective on life can change.

Happiness is doing something that you love to do because it promotes a feeling of well-being. It gives you a reason to get up in the morning, a feeling of goodness. Consider the opposite; just think of doing a job you hate; every day going to a place where you do not wish to be. It makes you depressed; it makes you sad and grumpy.

Happiness is being with friends, being with people you love. It gives you the feeling of being in harmony with the world. It is sharing happy times with those we love. When I was ill, my happiest moments were always the most simple. For me happiness was sharing time with friends, having a cup of coffee, sometimes outside in the sun. It was being with my family, sitting around the kitchen table chatting, laughing, just living moments, creating memories. It was walking along a beach staring at the expanse of ocean and trying to understand its vastness. It was walking in nature because nature to me is the door that creates peace in my inner sanctuary. Nature is all around us, it is always there to be enjoyed and it is free.

In conclusion, happiness is an inside job. It comes from deep within you.

The great essentials of happiness are, something to do, something to love and something to hope for.

(ALLAN K. CHALMERS)

A SENSE OF HUMOUR HELPS

Every survival kit should include a sense of humour

AUTHOR UNKNOWN

It can be a very difficult time going through any serious illness. But it helps to have a sense of humour and even laugh at yourself. It really can lighten the moment.

A few moments that made me smile were:

- My son had just started secondary school in September 2007. He came home one day and I was sitting at the kitchen table. He asked me, 'Mum, what is ekileksy?' I looked at him and said that I thought he must mean epilepsy. I told him what epilepsy was and asked him why he enquired. He told me that a boy in his class asked him if I had ekileksy and Jack had said, 'No, my mum has breast cancer' and the guy just answered 'Oh, right. That is different.' I truly smiled to myself.

- Every few weeks I had to wash my wig. My friend arrived in one day when I was putting on a wash, had the ironing board out and had my wig drying on my wig stand. She commented, 'You're some women to multi-task. You can put on a wash, iron and dry your hair at the same time.'

- My sister and I were strolling around a shopping centre one day and I followed her into a shop. Looking around, I realised that it was a shop for everything to do with hair – hair extension, brushes, hair dryers, tongs, etc. At this stage I had not a hair on my head. I looked at her and said, 'Claire, that was a brilliant idea, but it would help to have hair.' We laughed together.

- On another occasion, I was in the butcher's and the man behind the counter said that my hair was 'gorgeous', had I just come out of the hairdressers. What he was admiring was my wig. I replied that I had just come from getting my hair done and walked out of the shop grinning from ear to ear.

- My neighbour had a party and invited other neighbours, one of whom did not know that I had cancer. At this stage I was wearing my wig. When she walked in, she looked at me and asked if I was trying to make a fashion statement. I just smiled and said that I was. When she discovered I had cancer and was wearing a wig, she was mortified. I just laughed and actually got a kick out of it.

The benefits of laughter
- Laughter is good for our health.
- It relaxes the whole body.
- It boosts the immune system.
- It triggers the release of endorphins.
- It lifts our mood.
- It relieves stress.

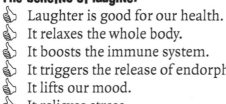

How to create opportunities to laugh
- Watch a funny movie or TV show
- Go to a children's concert – a school play at Christmas can be very funny
- Do something silly
- Be around funny people
- Go to a comedy show
- Check out your bookstore's humour section
- Laugh at yourself

WHAT I HAVE LEARNED

Lying in bed one day, I was pondering over the previous months and reflecting on my journey with cancer and what I had learned, particularly over the last three years.

This is a summary of the things that I have discovered about myself:

👍 It is important to have the right attitude and to stay positive.

👍 I brought a whole new meaning to optimism when I touched up my pink highlights just five days before I lost all my hair. I was going to enjoy them for the last time.

👍 I learned that looking good and making the effort with my appearance really did make me feel better

👍 Staying in the house and feeling sorry for myself was a complete waste of time, so when anyone invited me out for coffee I seized the opportunity and went –
   • a cup of coffee with a friend was a blessing and
   • another layer of dust would not kill anyone!

👍 Talking about my cancer really helped. It helped me and everyone around me.

👍 I counted my blessings. It is amazing what you see as blessings.

👍 It is a journey. Learn from it.

👍 I learned that your life can literally change in seconds.

👍 I really looked at nature. I saw the beauty all around me. The skies appeared bluer and the sun seemed to shine more often.

👍 I learned that I want to make a difference.

👍 I went for my chemo on a Tuesday. I particularly noticed that every Tuesday that I went, the sun shone. It does lift your heart.

- 👍 I stopped listening to bad news. I switched off the television. I decided I did not need it in my life.

- 👍 In your ordinariness, you can do extraordinary things.

- 👍 You have the power to change the world. You can be an inspiration.

- 👍 A good day is a brilliant day because you know how awful the bad days can be.

- 👍 If you lose your hair, it is highly traumatic. Don't listen to those who tell you it will grow back; they don't know what to say and they don't know what they are saying.

- 👍 Take risks, go for things, you might never get the chance again.

- 👍 I learned how lucky I was to have so much support.

- 👍 Don't be surprised if people go out of their way to avoid you. Don't take it personally – remember they have the problem, not you. They just don't know what to say.

- 👍 I decided I was only going to watch happy or funny films. I often just wanted to laugh.

- 👍 Whatever you find helps you, go for it.

- 👍 If you get tips from people, and believe you me you will get many, just take on board the ones that suit you.

- 👍 It is not a year out of your life. I decided it was a year in my life. How can you wipe out a whole year? Use it to learn, to grow, to explore, to reflect, to change, and to live.

- 👍 Relax and be – live in the moment.

- 👍 Friends and people are precious. Some are like stars, you may not always see them, but they are always there.

- 👍 Don't look back on your life with regrets.

- 👍 Remember, life is not perfect. To quote Leonard Cohen,

  > *There is a crack in everything*
  > *That is how the light gets in.*

- 👍 I learned a hard lesson when I discovered that cancer is an industry and there are people who will exploit your vulnerability, will have no conscience at taking your money and charging you exorbitant amounts for services.

- 👍 You have been given a second chance. Embrace it with both hands. Get out, live life, enjoy, smile, do things you would never have done before. It matters not what people think.

- 👍 Being courageous does not mean that you are not afraid. But it means that you are willing to keep going even when you are afraid.

- 👍 Develop the ability to see magic in the ordinary.

- 👍 I learned the gift of technology, by which I mean texting. When I was ill, it was always a joy to receive texts from friends. They were particularly welcome on the days when I did not feel well. I was grateful because, in those moments, I knew that that there was someone thinking of me.

SOME MEN'S PERSONAL STORIES

Because of my own particular cancer, I have generally met more women than men during my journey. When researching this book, however, I felt that it was also important to talk to men about their personal journeys through treatment for different cancers. These are their stories.

PETER'S STORY

Peter told me that originally his primary reason for going to his doctor was an in-grown toenail but he also had a troublesome mole/lump on his back and decided to ask the doctor to examine it. The doctor did not like the look of it and sent him immediately to a dermatologist who felt that it should be removed. He told Peter to come in the following morning as he had a cancelled appointment. In the process of removing the mole, the doctor quickly saw that it was more serious than initially suspected and referred him to a surgeon. He had a deep melanoma and there was the fear that it had spread so Peter had to have a PET scan. He was concerned, but thankfully the scan was all clear. This was a huge relief.

He says: 'I was shocked to hear that I had cancer, but from the very outset accepted the diagnosis. I put my faith in the medical team and believed that they would take care of me. The whole process, from my initial visit to the dermatologist and subsequently the surgeon, moved very quickly.'

He talked to his wife and she was always supportive right through his illness. However, Peter felt that some friends did not seem to comprehend that melanoma is actually cancer. He did not tell them at work for some time, since he was fearful that the competitors in his line of business would use the information to their own advantage. He worked right through his treatment because he felt that it kept his mind from dwelling on the enormity of the situation.

Peter believes that you cannot deny that you have had cancer. He would think about it most days, but not in a way that cripples his life and prevents him from moving forward. He is fearful of any unexpected pains. He believes that he has got a second chance, and for that he is grateful.

He says that he would have no problem talking to or helping anyone if they requested his help but feels that men are poor at communicating and believes that many people are too angry. Unlike a lot of men he did visit a cancer centre. He initially went for counselling at the Irish Cancer Society and also attended the course at the Cancer Centre, which he found to be extremely beneficial, as it was 'time out' for him. He felt guilty leaving work but realised that he needed it.

Peter likes the *Glastonbury Song* by the Water Boys in which there's a line 'I just found God where he always was'. His son was seven years old when Peter was diagnosed. One day, when browsing through the petition book in the hospital's oratory, Peter found the following, 'Please pray for my dad in room 106'. He was in room 106 and it was his son who wrote it. Peter was both touched and sad.

OSCAR'S STORY

Although there was a history of bowel cancer in his family, Oscar kept putting off the day to go for a colonoscopy. Eventually, after much gentle 'nagging' by his wife, he finally made the appointment. They discovered three tumours on his bowel; he had had no previous symptoms.

He told me: 'I didn't consider the actual test to be a huge ordeal but now think that it is vital that anyone with a family history of bowel cancer should be screened and would advise them to have it done.'

At the outset Oscar was numb, then asked 'Why me?' which was followed by 'Why not me?' After much thought, he decided to get on with it because he had no other option. He felt it was a matter of sink or swim. His family found it difficult, particularly his wife; he talked about his illness with his family.

He says: 'My brother had gone through the same treatment and it was really helpful to talk to him. However, I found that friends could not cope; in fact they avoided talking about it, as they did not know what to say. I've kept in touch with another man whom I met on the treatment and find that hugely beneficial.'

Oscar worked right through his chemotherapy and radiotherapy treatment. He had always worked very long hours in his job in the past and found that work really helped him. And yes, he would definitely talk to and try to help other people in a similar situation to himself.

'Cancer changed my life in that nothing will ever be the same again', he told me. 'In some ways the illness was liberating. If I'm in the company of people who get exercised over trivia, I just walk away and say that I don't have to listen to it.'

He says that he wouldn't go to a Cancer Support Centre. A friend wanted him to go to such a Centre, but it was not for Oscar. He believes we all have different coping strategies; he coped through his own determination to deal with his illness and the positive attitude of a wonderful cancer team. He had belief in his team that they were doing the best for him. When he was diagnosed, a whole system was put in place and carried out with utter professionalism. He felt very lucky and the sheer skill of the medical team in St James's and St Luke's hospitals filled him with confidence.

'I chose not to read about my illness because when I did so initially, I was reading about other people's problems and how they coped. I found that it was all so negative and decided that I did not need this information. Instead, I just analysed my own scenario, looked at how best to cope and just stuck to my own plan. But then everyone is different.'

Oscar did pray, not for himself but for his family. He decided to rely on his basic instinct that human intervention was the only factor in his survival. He has a nephew who is a spiritualist, a healer and believes in alternative remedies; he told him that grape seed oil would cure him. But Oscar thought this was a lot of rubbish and decided without hesitation that the surgeon's knife was his only option. He just wanted the tumours out.

After the treatment he did not get on too well because he had a temporary ileostomy which he found to be mentally and psychologically devastating. Only the thought of the promised reversion got him through this time. He adds, however, that if the ileostomy were a life-saving procedure that had to be permanent, he would have had to cope. The initial few days following the surgery were also difficult owing to the pain and the discomfort.

'I found that, mentally, dealing with the enormity of the operation was depressing at first but with the help of my family I got through it,' he says.

Oscar is doing very well, considering the seriousness of his cancer; he is getting on with his life. He is busy working and living life to the full.

JACK'S STORY

Late in 1994, while living in Toronto, Jack was suddenly and unexpectedly unable to pass urine but obtained relief when he attended the local hospital. A visit to a local Consultant resulted in tests and laser treatment but this was not successful in treating the problem of prostrate cancer.

Jack says: 'In June 1995, on returning to Dublin, I had a consultation with Mr David Hickey at Beaumont Hospital. Following necessary tests, he recommended an operation, which took place that August. He confirmed that the operation was very successful. However, I had to cope with incontinence for about a year and a half. To solve this problem, Dr Hickey recommended that I should have a consultation in Limerick with Dr Flood, who trained with him in the USA.'

Following consultations with Dr Flood and treatment in Limerick Regional Hospital, a sphincter was fitted to control the flow of urine, and life became comfortable again for Jack. He uses tena pads for added comfort. 'I pace myself in my activities and continue to enjoy life to the full at 83 years of age,' he says.

About ten years ago, Jack's GP asked him to join a group of his patients suffering from cancer on a visit to Lourdes. He agreed and says that it helped the patients to see how he had recovered. He also got a phone call from a priest living in Limerick, on the recommendation of Dr Flood, to discuss his anxiety about the cancer. Jack answered his questions and feels that the priest was happier after the phone conversation.

'Another priest, who is a friend for many years, had treatment for prostrate cancer in recent times', Jack told me. 'Knowing that I had experienced problems after my operation in the urine area, he was relieved to learn about the effectiveness of having a sphincter fitted. He took the same course of action as myself and it was very successful. Because of the success of my operation, I did not need any further treatment, such as chemotherapy.'

Jack says that his wonderful wife, Sighle, was and is a great tower of strength for him, and that he has always greatly appreciated family support.

PART 3
The Healing Journey

The best thing about the future is that it only comes one day at a time.

(ABRAHAM LINCOLN)

YOU HAVE JUST come through the journey of surgery, chemotherapy and radiotherapy. Now the healing journey begins.

One would think that when you finish your treatment you would be elated and delighted to have completed everything. You probably are, but the road forward can be fraught with anxiety and mixed feelings. It is quite difficult for anyone to understand, except someone who has gone through it, that in fact you are not quite feeling the way you thought you would feel. Instead, it is a complete anti-climax.

On the day I finished my chemotherapy, I remember walking out of the oncology room, a prescription in my hand, thinking, 'Is this it?' My sister was waiting for me and I just burst into tears. I did the same thing on the day that I finished my six weeks of radiotherapy. It is relief tinged with huge emotion. You have been so focused on getting through your treatment that you have not really stopped to think that you have had cancer. So for the first time, you are out of the treatment, out of the schedules of the hospital and you suddenly realise, I have had cancer. You are caught between relief at being finished and huge apprehension at trying to face the future. When you were going through your treatment, you had backup from the medical team and that security net has now been pulled away. It is completely normal to feel vulnerable but you do not expect it, and no one tells you that this is how you will probably feel.

Some people will say to you, 'Isn't it great now that you are back to normal?' They have no idea what they are saying. The fact is their 'normal' is never the same normal for you again. You have had cancer and your life has changed. I am not saying that it is a negative change but it has changed. I remember being rather fragile for many months after I finished my treatment. One of my recurring thoughts was what if the cancer returned and I lost my health again. This thought filled me with fear. I was feeling well and beginning to enjoy my life again but I was anxious and almost afraid to be happy. But these emotions and thoughts do pass.

Anniversaries can be silent reminders of times you would prefer to forget. The first anniversary is difficult. You are delighted to have come through the year but as you reflect back on it there can be many mixed feelings. I remember very vividly my first mammogram a year after my diagnosis. I felt really vulnerable and nervous; I had an uneasy feeling when I went through the hospital doors. It is not the actual mammogram but what it revealed a year previously. I felt everything would be ok but I was happy to get my results. The first anniversary is a milestone and I know I was extremely grateful to feel well.

So how do you now move on? Let me tell you what I did...

I finished all of my treatment in August 2008. My good friend Jack McArdle had been extremely good to me during my treatment. I had known Jack for many years but had lost touch for some time. One day while I was in the chemo room, he rang me out of the blue. He said he had been going through his address book and came across my name and decided to ring me to see how I was doing. When I told him where I was, he was genuinely surprised and from that day onwards he walked with me on the journey. At this particular time he was not too well himself, but we would meet and have a chat from time to time. The day after I finished all my treatment, I rang Jack and called to see him. He was so happy for me and told me I was going to be fine. I felt great hope. Unfortunately Jack has since passed away. I think of him a lot, as he was a writer and an inspiration to me.

My family and I had planned to go to the Canaries for a week just before Christmas. I really looked forward to this trip. Despite the weather being rather mixed, and two of my family being sick, I enjoyed the holiday so much. It was wonderful to be with them, away from hospitals and treatment.

The previous December, I had come out of hospital just five days before Christmas following my surgery. We got through Christmas but it was a difficult time, so I decided I wanted to do something different for Christmas 2008 and signed up as a volunteer to help with the homeless in the RDS, Dublin. My friend and my husband came with me. It was a wonderful, positive experience from which I got a lot more than I gave. It was a memorable Christmas Day.

In January 2009, I felt very well physically but was vulnerable both mentally and emotionally, so went for counselling to a Cancer Support Centre. My counsellor was ever so understanding and helped me a lot but a word of advice – go to a cancer centre for your counselling because they have so much experience in dealing with people who have come through cancer. I found that talking out my fears helped me to see things more clearly and I could move on with my life in a more clear and positive way. The feelings I had were completely normal, so don't feel frightened or a failure if you feel that way too.

The following month, I decided to do a Stress Management Course. Again this was held in the Cancer Centre and was really useful. I met others in a similar situation to myself. We had quite a small group and I looked forward to going every week. It was filled with good humour and positive vibes. We shared our journeys with each other. What you personally put into the course is what you will get out of the course.

There is much reflection during the time after treatment. Some people will get involved in support groups, some will become activists for cancer and some will just close the door and pretend it never happened. You choose your path and whatever you decide is right for you.

As time moved on, I became more confident and was able to enjoy my life in a different way. I believe now, nearly four years later, that life is for living. I feel I have been given a second chance and I'm not going to let this time slip through my fingers. I decided I was not going to be defined by my cancer. Do not let your cancer define you, but allow it to refine you or re-find you. By that I mean, do not let your cancer prevent you from living the rest of your life. This will take time because the recovery from cancer (or indeed from any serious illness) is a process. I cannot give you a time or a moment when I felt I had conquered this because it happens quite gradually; in fact, you often don't notice how well you are doing. I just know that each time I did something, it gave me the confidence to move forward again. One step led me to the next step. So here are some of the things I did....

I did a drumming workshop, which was just amazing. I sang with Christy Moore at a workshop. I was the guest speaker at a fundraising lunch to raise funds for a cancer support centre in Waterford. I walked a half marathon. I walked a full marathon. I did an advertisement for radio. I modelled at a breast cancer fashion show and I cannot let this opportunity go without telling you about it.

The Marie Keating Foundation has organised a fashion show for a number of years called 'Survive and Thrive' which takes place every October. It is run in conjunction with the Assets Modelling Agency and Irish Breast Care Nurses, and its aim is to show women that they can survive after breast cancer. Arnotts and Marks and Spencer provide the clothes. I had heard about it when researching this book. When I rang initially to enquire about it, they had their quota of people, so I just forgot about it but then I got a phone call about a month before the show asking me to participate. My husband drove me in to the Conrad Hotel on the day and I can remember saying to him that if I hadn't had cancer, I wouldn't be doing this. It is a strange contradiction. There were eighteen of us, all of whom had survived breast cancer. We were women in our thirties, forties, fifties and sixties. Size did not matter. I had to try on the four outfits that were allocated to me. We all had our make-up and hair done. We did a rehearsal before the show when Clara put us through our paces. There was a great buzz as the show started and that night we all felt like real celebrities. At the end, we walked out in single file and I felt truly emotional, remembering back to three years earlier when I was diagnosed. Little did I know then that three years later, almost to the month of diagnosis, I would be walking down a catwalk. Life is full of wonder and surprise.

The audience that night consisted of many people going through cancer treatment and I felt we were saying to them, in a non-verbal way, that this could be them up here on the stage next year. It was a wonderful night, terrifically empowering, and I would recommend anyone to take part. There is that feeling of 'I have conquered cancer'. My sister, Claire, and my daughter Emma, were both in the audience and thoroughly enjoyed the night.

A brief addendum ... the following morning, I received a text from a friend that read, 'I suppose you won't get out of bed for less than €10,000 a day'. I texted back, 'Of course not. All enquiries through my agent please'.

If I get an opportunity to do something now, I never turn it down because it might not come my way again. I definitely take more risks and am not as fearful of taking on challenges.

HOW DOES THE HEALING BEGIN?

A survivor's care plan is for the future.
An empowering reminder that you still have control of your life.
Cancer happened to you but it does not have to define who you are.

(KAREN KARLS)

There are so many factors involved in making a recovery from illness. It is another stage of the journey. No one tells you that you may feel low emotionally and it comes as a shock when you are not elated. But if you think about it, it has been a journey of survival up to now and your whole recovery after treatment is a process. In fact, your recovery may take a lot longer than your treatment did. For life to move forward, you have to find a new way to cope. Some people may think that by ignoring what has happened to them is the best way to get over it and move on. In my opinion that is not the way to go. You can't just forget that you have had cancer because you may still be suffering from side-effects from the treatment, which are a constant reminder of what you have been through. Some problems will disappear quickly, but others may remain for weeks, months or longer.

Try to surround yourself with good support systems, family and friends. Take personal responsibility for your mind, body and spirit. You may decide to take more exercise each week. You may decide to do a yoga class or some kind of relaxation class. Meditation is a wonderful resource.

If you cannot feel yourself getting a lift or if you feel depressed, you may need medical help. You could go to your GP for guidance and/or go to counselling if you feel that talking to a professional may help. The Cancer Support Centres are a wonderful resource because they have experience in understanding how you feel at this time. There are also complimentary therapies available through these centres. You are offered four treatments and if you have not availed of them during your chemotherapy, perhaps now would be a good time to treat yourself, as they can be both relaxing and therapeutic. Be kind to yourself. You have been through a tough period and you need time to heal.

WORRYING ABOUT A RECURRENCE

Worrying about a cancer reoccurrence is completely normal, especially in the year following treatment. Some people are paralysed by fear of the cancer returning. A pain that would have gone unnoticed prior to cancer can now become a cause of major anxiety. It is difficult for anyone who has not been through cancer to understand but there is a certain security when you are going through your treatment that the cancer is under control; you have the belief that nothing can happen. You are also in regular contact with the medical team and that brings great reassurance. When the treatment is over, that is gone and you feel on your own. So here are some tips that may help:

- Make sure you attend all your follow-up appointments. If you have scans, mammograms or any form of tests, always get your results. Never assume that they are clear, even if no one gets back to you with the results.
- You should find out:
  – What tests you need and how often?
  – Where do you attend for these tests?
  – Do you personally have to make these appointments?

HAVING A PURPOSE IN LIFE

There is nothing like having a brush with death or being told you have a life-threatening illness to make you sit up and assess what is important in life. This is your chance to take a serious look at where you are going.

There is no doubt that it takes courage to live in a way that makes life worthwhile after being diagnosed with cancer. It takes courage, because if life is worth living, then there is a lot to lose. Some people seize life with both hands while others become very cautious and full of fear. According to evidence and from my own experience, the people who are around longer are those who make plans, set goals and generally make life worthwhile, no matter what their diagnosis. Their glass is always half-full.

THE BENEFITS OF SETTING GOALS

If you wish to pursue good health, you should pay attention to your needs, whether physical, emotional or spiritual. Try to put measures into place, that will ensure that you regain good health. One of the most effective ways of taking positive action is to set some life goals. It is important that you focus on your reason for living, on what you want to give and to receive from life now. Setting goals has many benefits: -

- It prepares you mentally and emotionally for your commitment to regain full health – you expect to recover.

- It expresses confidence in your ability to meet those goals.

- It gives you the sense of being in charge of your life and builds a positive image; and

- It provides a focus for establishing priorities.

Goal-setting techniques

- Write down your goals and make them specific.
- Make them measurable – chart your progress as you head towards your goal.
- Make them attainable.
- Make them realistic.
- Set a time limit.
- Make them within your power to happen.
- Remember that it's ok to dream and then work out the practicalities.

Set out goals for three months, six months and one year. Have fun in setting them out and consider how you are going to achieve them.

SO WHAT WILL YOU DO NOW?

> Your life is a sacred journey, and it is about change, growth, discovery, movement, transformation, continuously expanding your vision of what is possible, stretching your soul, learning to see clearly, deeply, listening to your intuition, taking courageous challenges at every step along the way. You are on the path ... exactly where you are meant to be right now ... and from here, you can only go forward, shaping your life story into a magnificent tale of triumph, of healing, of courage, of beauty, of wisdom, of power, of dignity and of love.

(CAROLINE ADAMS)

You walk this journey in your own unique way. We all have different coping mechanisms. You have your own perspective and you will view this time through your lens. There is no right or wrong way; just your way. So what can you do? What aspirations or hopes have you fostered in your life? What did you always wish to do? Maybe now is the time to follow your dreams. Maybe now is the time to take care of you. Maybe now this is your time. I was asked the question recently, 'What makes your heart sing?' This may be a question worthy of reflection for you.

You have come through cancer and your life has changed. It is up to you how you will take on this challenge. You had a choice when you first got your cancer. Now you have another choice – to move forward or to stop living your life. You can accept it, learn, grow and see it as an opportunity to do the best you can with the rest of your life.

Learning to embrace change can be a life-enriching experience. Perhaps your illness, how you move on and what you have learned, holds the key to tomorrow, your future. Every day is a chance to change your life. Every day is a blank page – a new beginning. Don't let the fear of failure prevent you from doing new things. I believe that there are no mistakes because you learn from everything. When I set out on the journey with cancer, I probably faced a challenge that I would never have thought could happen to me. I know I looked fear in the eye, but from that experience I have gained strength, courage and confidence. The following words by John O'Donohue had a profound effect on my attitude to my illness.

> May you find the wisdom to listen to your illness;
> Ask it why it came? Why it chose your friendship?
> Where it wants to take you? What it wants you to know?
> What quality of space it wants to create in you?
> What you need to learn to become more fully yourself
> That your presence may shine in the world?

Yes, of course a cancer diagnosis is a shock but you can get through it. I do not say that lightly. But just remember that cancer cannot take away your sense of humour; it cannot silence your laughter – only if you allow it.

My daughter talked to me about a wonderful concept called 'pay it forward'. Consider all the people who have helped you on your cancer journey and how you can now keep this kindness going. The people who supported you may not wish to be thanked, but there are always ways to give back, to help someone else and 'pay it forward'.

I saw a quote once that said, 'The future looks so bright, I have to wear shades'. That is my wish for your future – that you grasp every moment, that you step out in hope and that you have a bright future. Hope is that knock on the door of your heart, which says 'You can do it'.

For Your Information

Some of the Cancer Support Centres have courses to help people when their treatment is completed. If you think that it would be beneficial to seek help in this way, it is worthwhile contacting your nearest Cancer Centre to enquire if they have such a course.

LARCC in Mullingar has a residential week to support people after treatment.

There is a book called *The Healing Journey* by Dr. Alastair Cunningham, who had cancer himself and understands the journey of recovering from cancer and getting on with your life. It is available to everyone free of charge by downloading the workbooks and mp3 files from the Internet at the following websites:

www.healingjourney.ca/resource.htm
www.healingjourney.org.uk/resources

You can also buy the workbooks and audios by mail order. The material will take you through a series of step by step progressive sessions that include coping skills such as relaxation, healthy thought management, guided imagery, journaling, meditation and other self-help strategies.

A SPACE TO PAUSE AND REFLECT

At the centre of your being, you have the answer.

(LAO TZU)

Only when the clamour of the outside world is silenced will you be able to hear the deeper vibration. Listen carefully.

(SARAH BAN BREATHNACH)

Throughout my life, I have always sought quiet places, a spiritual space where I could escape, nurture and feed my soul. I did not know way back then that the time spent in the embrace of those sanctuaries of peace would give me strength and a feeling of well-being right through my cancer journey.

There are many places in Ireland where it is possible to take time out for reflection, meditation, time for you to stop and pause. These include:

Glenstal Abbey, Murroe, County Limerick
Jampa Ling, County Cavan
Sunyata Retreat Centre, County Clare
Kalyana Centre, County Kerry
Holy Hill Hermitage, County Sligo
Dzogchenbeara, County Cork
Passaddhi, County Cork
Glencomeragh House (Rosminians), Kilsheelan,
    County Tipperary
An Tearmann, Glendalough, County Wicklow
The Sanctuary, Dublin 7
Glendalough Hermitage Centre, Glendalough,
    County Wicklow

Glenstal Abbey, County Limerick

Glenstal is a Benedictine Monastery set in a 500-acre estate. The Abbey is home to a community of monks. Liturgical prayer is central to the life of the monks. Benedictine worship emphasises beauty, harmony and celebrates God's presence. Glenstal welcomes people of all denominations or none – anyone who is walking the spiritual path.

The Guest House at Glenstal Abbey is a facility for those who want to spend some prayerful days in a monastic setting. Those who come are invited to attend the liturgies in the abbey church, which take place several times each day. Meals are provided and, if any guest desires some spiritual guidance, this can be arranged. The Guest House features twelve ensuite rooms. Occasionally, the Guest House welcomes groups, but for the most part, people come as individuals and so more easily absorb the atmosphere, which is provided by monastic space.

For further information and bookings:
Tel. 061 386103
Email: guestmaster@glenstal.org
www.glenstal.org

Jampa Ling, Bawnboy, County Cavan

Jampa Ling is a residential retreat centre in north-west Cavan, set in thirteen acres of meadow, woodland and gardens, under the guidance and spiritual direction of Panchen Ötrul Rinpoche. Jampa Ling is open to visitors, both Buddhist and those of other traditions (or none). Aside from organised retreats and events, many people come to Jampa Ling to enjoy its peaceful ambience and beautiful natural surroundings. Guests are free to join in with the morning and evening meditations, browse in the Buddhist library, and explore the grounds and environs.

Prices (includes all meals): Dormitory accommodation, €36 per person; Double room, €36 per person or €45 for a single occupancy

Solitary Retreat Facility

There is also a facility available for those wishing to pursue a solitary retreat in a mobile-home situated in a quiet and secluded part of the grounds. This provides a supportive and peaceful environment in which to conduct a retreat and has been set aside specifically for solitary retreatants.

Price: €20 per night; electricity is charged separately.

For further information and bookings:
Jampa Ling, Owendoon House, Bawnboy, County Cavan
Tel. 049 952 3448
Email: info@jampaling.org

Sunyata Retreat Centre, Sixmilebridge, County Clare

Sunyata is a beautiful 10-acre property in the rolling hills of east County Clare. A spacious haven away from the bustle of modern life, Sunyata is perfectly situated for relaxation, meditation, and contemplation. Sunyata's main connection is with the Thai forest tradition of Theravada Buddhism, and their main practice is mindfulness meditation. Sunyata is open to people of any faith and to all the traditions in Buddhism. Sunyata has weekly Wednesday night meditations, offer their own programme of retreats, and has occasional opportunities for personal retreats when no retreat is scheduled.

For further information and bookings:
Sunyata Retreat Centre, Snata, Sixmilebridge, County Clare
Tel. 061 36773
Email: Info@sunyatacentre.com
www.sunyatacentre.com

Kalyana Centre, Dingle Peninsula, County Kerry

Kalyana Centre for Mindfulness is located on the Dingle Peninsula, close to Mount Brandon. The Centre is located at the mouth of the stunning Moc a Na Bo valley in a beautifully renovated farmhouse and barn, surrounded by gardens. Kalyana offers Mindfulness Meditation, Mindfulness-Based Stress Reduction and gentle voice work. In addition to a programme of group retreats (see website), Kalyana also offers facilities for individual self-retreat and time out.

Guests are welcome to come for a day, a week, or longer. Meditation instruction or guidance is available. Accommodation is offered in the Garden Cabin, a delightful, warm, turf roofed meditation cabin located at the top of the garden, with extensive mountain views and a glimpse of the sea.

Price: €30 single, €50 double per night. Dinner €15

For further information and bookings:

Kalyana Centre for Mindfulness

40 John Street, Dingle, County Kerry

Tel. 087-2712662

Emaileva@kalyanacentre.com

www.kalyanacentre.com

Holy Hill Hermitage, Screen, County Sligo

Holy Hill Hermitage is home to a small community of men and women who live as apostolic hermits according to the Carmelite tradition. They are part of the Spiritual Life Institute, a community dedicated to simplicity of life, contemplative prayer, and apostolic outreach.

The Community at Holy Hill welcomes anyone who wants to make a private retreat for a day, a week, or longer, or to come for extended sabbatical time. People making a longer retreat stay in a beautiful, private hermitage. Basic foods are provided. Spiritual direction is available. There is also one hermitage (a small cottage) available for couples that want to come on retreat together.

Price/ suggested donation: €55 for the first night and €50 for each additional night. Full week €300 euros.

For further information and bookings:

Holy Hill, Skreen, County Sligo

Tel. 071-9166021

Email holyhill@eircom.net

www.holyhill.ie

Dzogchenbeara, County Cork

Dzogchenbeara is a Tibetan Buddhist Retreat Centre under the spiritual direction of Sogyal Rinpoche, author of *The Tibetan Book of Living and Dying*.

Many people visit Dzogchenbeara simply to enjoy a break from their busy lives. They find that the atmosphere of spiritual practice, together with the seclusion and natural surroundings, provide an ideal environment for rest and reflection, healing and renewal. The Centre's cottages and farmhouse hostel are open to anyone who would like to spend some time in the environment of the retreat centre.

For further information and bookings:
Dzogchenbeara, Garranes, Allihies, West Cork
Tel. 027 73032
Email: info@dzogchenbeara.org
www.dzogchenbeara.org

Passaddhi, Beara Way, Beara Peninsula, County Cork

Passaddhi is a small meditation centre in the Beara Peninsula which seeks to make the teachings of the Buddha, and in particular the meditation practices of vipassana and metta, available to as many people as possible, whether they are Buddhist or non-Buddhist.

In addition to group retreats (see website for details), there is a chalet on site called kuti, in the Buddhist tradition of Thailand and Burma, which can be used for personal retreats, with a minimum stay of two nights.

Resident Teacher Marjó will be able to offer guidance and support if you don't have an established meditation practice yet and would like to start one. If you have an established practice, you're welcome to use the chalet. It can be rented on a self-catering basis or Marjó can provide vegetarian meals.

Price/donation: The kuti is offered on a donation basis, with a guideline of an amount per night in accordance with the price of a local B&B, and a donation for food and additional expenses. The kuti sleeps two.

For further information and bookings:

Tel. 027 60223

Email: moosterhoff@eircom.net

www.Vipassana.ie

Glencomeragh House (Rosminians), Kilsheelan, County Tipperary

The House of Prayer sits at the foot of the Comeragh Mountains looking out over the valley of the River Suir. There are a variety of forest walks, countryside rambles and mountain hills, all easily accessible. Accommodation includes 16 single and four double rooms, and four Hermitages.

Price: Full board from €80 daily. Self-catering from €60 single and €80 double nightly.

For further information and bookings:

Tel: 052 613 3181

Email: info@glencomeragh.ie

Tearmann Spirituality Centre, Glendalough, Co. Wicklow

An Tearmann is a sacred space in the heart of Glendalough. It offers six-day retreats and weekends, and is ideal for small groups working together for a few days. Also available by arrangement are one-to three-month stays and walkabouts for groups.

Price: Single room, €45; double room, €65

For further information and bookings:

Tel. Michael Rodgers, SPS 0404 45208 or Breda Ahearn, C.P. 0404 45639 Email micr@eircom.net

www.tearmann.ie

The Sanctuary, Stanhope Street, Dublin 7

The Sanctuary is an oasis of peace in the heart of Dublin city. It was born out of the Christian tradition, but it is open to people of all faiths, respecting and embracing the richness of diversity. It is grounded in the belief that mindful living is the key to a balanced life. It offers courses, programmes and workshops all year round. There is a beautiful garden, which is a place of rest and calm for the mind, body and spirit. Meditation and stillness are central to the ethos of the Sanctuary. Meditation is seen in the Sanctuary as the art of Being Still, Being Aware, Being Present, Being Grounded, Being in the NOW.... Being.

For further information and bookings:
Tel. 01 670 5419
Email: enquiries@sanctuary.ie

Glendalough Hermitage Centre, Glendalough, Co. Wicklow

Glendalough rests high up in the Dublin Mountains. It is renowned for its beauty, peace and tranquil surroundings. The Glendalough Hermitage Centre is an oasis of silence and solitude.

For further information and bookings:
Tel: 0404 45571, MOB: 087 935 6696
Email: glendalough2000@eircom.net
www.hermitage.dublindiocese.ie

THIS IS MY WISH FOR YOU

Hope to not lose heart
Light to show you the way
Strength on difficult days
Courage to keep going
Patience when you feel like giving up
Friends to walk with you
Beauty for your eyes to see
Laughter to make you smile
Faith when you doubt
A hug when your heart is heavy
An angel to guide you
The belief that you can make a difference
Wisdom to stop and reflect
Silence to touch your soul
Confidence to believe in yourself
Perseverance when you might quit
The gift of believing that
The rest of your life awaits you.

Cathy McCarthy

REFLECTIONS by John O'Donohue

For Courage
When the light around you lessens
And your thoughts darken until
Your body feels fear turn
Cold as a stone inside.

When you find yourself bereft
Of any belief in yourself
And all you unknowingly
Leaned on has fallen.

When one voice commands
Your whole heart
And it is raven dark.

Steady yourself and see
That it is your own thinking
That darkens your world,
Search and you will find
A diamond thought of light,

Know that you are not alone
And that this darkness has purpose;
Gradually it will school your eyes
To find the one gift your life requires
Hidden within this night-corner.

Invoke the learning
Of every suffering
You have suffered.

Close your eyes.
Gather all the kindling
About your heart.
To create one spark.
That is all you need.
To nourish the flame
That will cleanse the dark
Of its weight of festered fear.

A new confidence will come alive
To urge you towards higher ground
Where your imagination
Will learn to engage difficulty
As its most rewarding threshold!

A Blessing for a Friend on the Arrival of Illness

Now is the time of dark invitation
Beyond a frontier you did not expect;
Abruptly, your old life seems distant.

You barely noticed how each day opened
A path through fields never questioned,
Yet expected, deep down, to hold treasure.
Now your time on earth becomes full of threat;
Before your eyes your future shrinks.

You lived absorbed in the day to day.
So continuous with everything around you,
That you could forget you were separate;

Now this dark companion has come between you,
Distances have opened in your eyes,
You feel that against your will
A stranger has married your heart.

Nothing before has made you
Feel so isolated and lost.

When the reverberations of shock subside in you,
May grace come to restore you to balance.
May it shape a new space in your heart
To embrace this illness as a teacher
Who has come to open your life to new worlds.

May you find in yourself
A courageous hospitality
Towards what is difficult,
Painful and unknown.

May you learn to use this illness
As a lantern to illuminate
The new qualities that will emerge in you.

May the fragile harvesting of this slow light
Help to release whatever has become false in you.
May you trust this light to clear a path
Through all the fog of old unease and anxiety
Until you feel arising within you a tranquillity
Profound enough to call the storm to stillness.

May you find the wisdom to listen to your illness;
Ask it why it came? Why it chose your friendship?
Where it wants to take you? What it wants you to
    know?
What quality of space it wants to create in you?
What you need to learn to become more fully
    yourself
That your presence may shine in the world?

May you keep faith with your body,
Learning to see it as a holy sanctuary
Which can bring this night-wound gradually
Towards the healing and freedom of dawn.

May you be granted the courage and vision
To work through passivity and self-pity,
To see the beauty you can harvest
From the riches of this dark invitation.

May you learn to receive it graciously,
And promise to learn swiftly
That it may leave you newborn,
Willing to dedicate your time to birth

If I Had My Life to Live Over
Bottom of Form

If I had my life to live over
I would dare to make more mistakes next time.
I would relax, limber up.
I would be sillier than I have been this trip.
I would take fewer things seriously and take more
chances.
I would climb more mountains, swim more rivers, and
watch more sunsets.
I would be crazier.
I would be less hygienic.
I would take more trips.
I would eat more ice cream and fewer beans.
I would, perhaps, have more actual troubles but I would
have fewer imaginary ones.

You see, I am one of those people who live sanely, sensibly,
prudently;
hour after hour, day after day.
Oh, I have had my moments!
And if I had to do it over again, I would have more of
them.
Maybe I would have nothing else?
Just moments, one after another, instead of living so many
years ahead of each day.
I have been one of those people who never goes anywhere
without a thermometer,
a hot water bottle, a raincoat, and a parachute.

If I had it to do it over, I would travel lighter on the next
trip.
I would start going barefoot earlier in the spring and stay
that way later in the fall.
I wouldn't make such good grades, except by accident.
I would have more sweethearts.

I would go to more dances.
I would sing more songs and play more games.
I would ride more merry-go-rounds.
I'd pick more daisies.

If I had my life to live over.

Nadine Starr – 85 years old

Cathy and Emer, Dublin City Marathon, 25th October 2010

PART 4

A Little Bit of Escapism

FOUND DURING my cancer journey that particular books and films helped me through some difficult days.

I list below some suggestions that others and I enjoyed. I did not pick anything too challenging. Rather, I selected films and books to help you escape and forget everything for a while.

Films:

Enchanted

The Devil Wears Prada

Sex in the City 1 and 2

Maid in Manhattan

The Holiday

P.S. I Love You

Mamma Mia

Pretty Woman

Bridget Jones' Diary

The Wedding Planner

Julie & Julia

What a Girl Wants

Sweet Home Alabama

Working Girl

A Good Year

August Rush

Ghost

Oceans 11

Regarding Henry

Big Daddy

How to Lose a Guy in 10 Days

Shall we Dance?

Legally Blonde

Two Weeks' Notice

Notting Hill

The Ugly Truth

It's Complicated

Just Like Heaven

Marley and Me

Miss Congeniality

My Fair Lady

My Big Fat Greek Wedding

Sabrina

Roman Holiday

Under the Tuscan Sun

Jumping Jack Flash

Cool Runnings

The Pelican Brief

The Bucket List

What Women Want

Scent of a Woman
Indecent Proposal
As Good as it Gets
Shirley Valentine

The Usual Suspects
Cheaper by The Dozen
Lucky 7

Books

Angels in My Hair, Lorna Byrne
Eat Pray Love, Elizabeth Gilbert
Jodi Picoult's Books
Any of the Chicken Soup Books*
*Benedictus,** John O'Donohue
The Funniest Things You Never Said, Rosemarie Jarski
The Cancer Vixen, Marisa Acocella Marchetto
The Secret Life of Bees, Sue Monk Kidd
The Rules of Life, Richard Templar
*Dear Sebastian,** Christine Horgan
*Sonas: Celtic Thoughts on Happiness,** Catherine Conlon
That They May Face the Rising Sun, John McGahern
One Step Beyond, Chris Moon
*Now Is The Time: Spiritual Reflections,** Sr. Stanislaus Kennedy
*Footprints on the Path,** Eileen Caddy

* I often found it difficult to read, as I could not concentrate. I found it helpful to have some books that I could just dip into; no huge commitment and some of these books were good for my soul.

While doing research for my own book, I found the following books helpful:
Love, Medicine and Miracles, Bernie Siegel, M.D.
Getting Well Again, O. Carl Simonton, M.D.,
        Stephanie Matthews-Simonton
44½ Choices you can make if you have Cancer,
        Sheila Dainow, Vicki Golding and Jo Wright
Even the Eyebrows, Sharon Morrison

Creative Visualisation, Shakti Gawain
Cancer: 50 Essential Things to Do, Greg Anderson
What Can I Do to Help? Deborah Hutton
The Green Beauty Bible, Sarah Stacey & Josephine Fairley
You Can Get Through This, Domini Stuart
What's Really in your Basket? Bill Statham
Look Good Feel Good, Rhona Cullinan with
        the Irish Academy of Beauty

GIFT IDEAS FOR A FRIEND

Some people are at a loss to know what to buy someone with cancer. I came across a story on line about one woman getting a present of a cat during her chemotherapy – this is not what I would recommend! Below are some suggestions to guide you or others.

- A nice journal, notebook or diary – e.g. *The Irish Get Up and Go Diary* – described as a diary with a difference – it can be purchased at ***www.getupandgodiary.com***).
- A voucher for a nice café
- DVDs or books (see separate list)
- An audio book – if you are too tired to read, an audio book could help
- Subscription for a newspaper or magazine
- Organic shower gels, shampoo, hand cream (see suggestions in section, 'A More Natural Beauty')
- Oils (A More Natural Beauty)
- An Angel (The Willow Tree has an interesting range – available in Gift Shops)
- Slippers, bathrobe, pyjamas – cheerful colours
- Book of crosswords, quizzes, word searches
- Voucher for a beauty treatment
- Meditation CD
- Voucher for a personal shopper (an idea for a few

friends – see list in 'Dress Like Today Matters')
- Nuts, seeds, dried fruit (a neighbour used to bring me these from time to time and it was a nice, useful snack)
- A small posy of gently scented flowers, such as freesia, daffodils, sweet pea
- A voucher for a night away (possible suggestion for a group)

Useful Websites

www.breastcancer.org
www.cancerhelp.org.uk
www.cancercare.org
www.chemocare.com
www.nationalcancerinstitute.com
www.canceraustralia.gov.au
www.breastcancercare.org.uk
www.cancerselfcare.com
www.ewg.org
www.sloanekettering.com
www.mayoclinic.com
www.livestrong.com
www.cincovidas.com
www.about.com
www.naturallysafe.com.au
www.cancernutritioninfo.com
www.healingjourney.org.uk
www.irishcancersociety.ie
www.macmillan.org.uk
www.pennybrohncancercare.org
www.quantumpsychotherapy.com
www.cancer.org
www.101WaysSeries.com
www.whfoods.com
www.cancercouncil.com

APPENDIX 1

AFTER THE TREATMENT FINISHES – THEN WHAT?

By Dr. Peter Harvey,
Consultant Clinical Psychologist,
Leeds Teaching Hospitals Trust

D R PETER HARVEY gave the following talk at the Annual Conference of the Cancer Self-Help Groups in England. He is truly grateful to them as they gave him a forum to express his ideas. This talk captures well how you feel when the treatment is all over.

"Imagine a roller-coaster. Some of you will find this an exciting and thrilling image: others of you – like me – will find it terrifying and beyond belief that anyone in their right mind would willingly subject themselves to the torment of being transported at high speed and with great discomfort in this manner. However, I have chosen this image to represent the process of the diagnosis and treatment of cancer. On a roller-coaster, you will be strapped in and sent off into the terror, knowing that there is nothing you can do about it until you emerge, wobbly and battered at the other end. You manage by getting your head down and dealing with it as best you can at the time. It is only afterwards, when you are on solid ground again, that you can look back with amazement and view what you have experienced and marvel at your courage.

This seems to be an analogy for what happens after diagnosis and during treatment. The end of the ride is equivalent to the end of treatment. And this is where I want to start – after the treatment has finished and at the point where you can begin, bit-by-bit, to deal with all that you have been through and all that is to come. You may have had to endure months of treatment by knife, chemicals or radiation until you are probably sick of the whole business, both literally and metaphorically. Now is the time to heal, both body and mind. What I hope to do is to look in more detail at this process and make a plea that this critical stage is given more attention than it has had in the past.

I want to set out a framework in which to develop an understanding of what is happening. The first part of this framework is the recovery process that has to be gone through. For me this happens in three stages: recuperation, convalescence and rehabilitation. I make this distinction to represent the different stages that have to be passed through and completed before moving on to the next one – each builds upon the other, although there will not necessarily be a clear dividing line between them.

Let's look at each of these in turn, beginning with recuperation. It is a widely held belief, often correct, that the treatment of an illness is meant to make you feel better. One of the many paradoxes of cancer is that, more often than not, the treatment makes you feel worse. This is not surprising. We cut and possibly mutilate, inject you with poisonous and powerful chemicals, subject you to dangerous rays all in the name of treatment. The aggressiveness and power of the treatments are a necessary response to the power of the disease, of course, but this very power takes its toll in other ways. These interventions place enormous physical strains on the body. There is often little time to recover from one treatment before the next one starts. The treatments themselves may make it difficult for you to sleep and eat properly – two important parts of the body's defence and recovery system. Some of the treatments drain your energy and resources to such an extent that it's as much as you can do to put on the kettle. Add to this the emotional turmoil – the dealing with the impact and implications of the diagnosis, the uncertainty, the upheaval, the additional burden that you feel that you are imposing on family and friends, the loss of so many aspects of your routine. Emotional stress can be as energy-consuming as any physical activity. After all that, is it any wonder that you feel wrung out and exhausted, without resources or reserves? All too often I meet people who, for quite understandable reasons, want to get back to doing the things they used to before the diagnosis but find themselves falling at the first hurdle because they simply find the whole thing too much. In my view, however smoothly your treatment has progressed and however well you have tolerated the various indignities to which we subject you, some time simply to recharge and recover – to recuperate – is absolutely essential. This is the necessary foundation on which to build recovery. There is no one right way or length of time to do this. It may be a few days or a few weeks – how long will depend on your state of health before your diagnosis, your age, the intensity, frequency and length of your treatment and so on. Take however long you feel you need. Recuperating is the very first step in a process of rebuilding.

The next stage is convalescence. This is a rather old-fashioned term, and I am sorry it has fallen into disuse, despite its association with bath chairs, rugs, the seaside and strengthening broth. The word has a Latin root meaning "to grow strong" – rather apt under the circumstances. Once you have recharged your batteries, then you can begin to build up your physical and emotional strength. Again, there are no set rules or guidelines for how long this can take, but I firmly believe that to miss out this stage builds up problems later on.

Once you have recuperated and convalesced, then you have the foundation and the energy to start doing those things that you want to do – and, perhaps, to stop doing those things that you don't want to do. I remember the patient of a colleague of mine who, once she had completed her treatment for her breast cancer, asked for help to '...

sort out her job, her marriage and her cancer – and in that order'. After eight sessions, she had decided to change both job and husband. Now your rehabilitation may not be as dramatic or as quick as that, but behind that rather clinical term lies a whole raft of important issues. Perhaps one of the most critical of these concerns the phrase 'Getting back to normal'. I will argue that, if taken too literally, it can be more of a hindrance than a help and may become a burden which impedes progress. My reason for taking this stand is based on the observation that once heard, the diagnosis of cancer can never be forgotten. Whatever your prognosis, whatever your hopes, whatever your personality, the second that you know that you have cancer your life changes irrevocably. For many people, their sense of security and safety is undermined, their hopes for the future compromised, their trust in their world denied. I will return to the process of dealing with that threat later on, but for now I simply want to acknowledge that to 'get back to normal' as if nothing has happened is an unlikely hope. But of course, within that phrase lie a number of other aspirations and messages.

The whole process from diagnosis, through treatment to completion, is entirely and utterly abnormal. For months your life is taken over by what must seem like an endless stream of clinic visits, of being prodded and poked, scanned and punctured, of waiting and watching, of hopes realised and hopes dashed. Your life has been taken over by others, run to someone else's timetable. There is every reason for wanting to get back to something that is yours to control, yours to manage, back to something familiar. However, to try to do that when so much has changed is a difficult, if not impossible task. The trick is how to regain control and stability in a changed world. Rehabilitation, therefore, is a process of regaining and refreshing old skills, leaning and refining new ones to enable you to live the sort of life you want. So what are the tasks that have to be completed in order to get through the process that I have outlined?

Regaining trust in your body

For many of you, your cancer will have been discovered whilst you were feeling well and healthy – either through some sort of screening programme, through investigations for other illness or for a relatively innocuous symptom. You may have had few – if any – times when you felt ill or have very troubling symptoms (I know this is not true for all, but it is a common experience nonetheless). And then you hear the diagnosis, that word that will be forever etched in your memory. How is it possible to have the disease that so many dread without feeling sick? This is another of the many paradoxes of cancer. Surely if you are ill then you should feel ill? This doesn't last long however, because you then start treatment – and for most people that's when they start feeling ill. All the treatments change your body in one way or another, sometimes permanently and often for a period of time that lasts much longer than the treatment itself.

One of the consequences of all this is that you may lose faith in your ability to recognise when something is wrong with your body. After all, you may not have been able to tell that you had cancer in the first place and your body is now significantly changed, so that there is a whole set of new and unusual sensations to experience. This is most marked in the period after treatment when the anxieties are still high and the uncertainty at a peak. Is this lump the cancer coming back? What does that pain mean? Should I go back to the clinic, just in case? Such anxieties are perfectly understandable under the circumstances. The rules have changed and you need to learn a new way of handling the aches and pains, lumps and bumps that you would not have given second thoughts to before all this started. This will all be made worse by a perceptual bias and hypersensitivity to these changes. You will be on the lookout for them in a way that you were not before. This is a combination of doing what you have probably been told to do by the staff and your own real anxieties and fears.

Previously insignificant and benign bodily changes become magnified and interpreted as a result of your immediate past experience. It is important to keep this in check and to give yourself some guidelines to manage your fears. For example, if the pain lasts for more than a couple of days or gets worse, if there are symptoms associated with the site of your surgery for more than a certain length of time, only then might you need to call your doctor. Your consultant and specialist nurse will be able to give you guidance as to what they think will be important. Whilst many people quite naturally, and over time, learn to manage this unpleasant and frightening experience, some will not, especially if you have always been a 'bit of a worrier' about your health. In this case, I think it important that you have very open conversations with your consultant, your GP and specialist nurse about how you can access expert reassurance quickly and without having the sense of being a nuisance. Just as you have learned about your body whilst you were growing up, so you can re-learn about it in later life.

Regaining trust in yourself

I cannot tell you how many people, from all walks of life, have told me that one of the most difficult consequences of their illness and its treatment is their loss of confidence. It seems to make no difference if you are a woman or a man, old or young, have a high-powered, demanding job or are retired. Cancer is a great leveller in this (as in many other) respects. Of course one of the great problems with confidence is that no-one else can give it to you: you cannot get your doctor to write a prescription or buy it in a bottle from Sainsbury's. You gain confidence by doing things and developing your sense of self-confidence – but how do you start when you are not confident enough? It's very easy to get trapped in a self-defeating and immobilising loop from which there seems to be no escape. Exactly why this should happen is not entirely clear. Part of it is probably due to the sense of uncontrollability and the experience of powerlessness that cancer and its treatment engenders.

Another factor that will undoubtedly contribute is the sense that the world is not a safe place any more – that you are vulnerable and at risk is brought home to you with a terrible certainty. This can manifest itself in a number of ways, but one that seems very potent concerns holidays. Many people have the idea that what would be really nice at the end of treatment is a real holiday. You or your relatives may plan to have a break very soon after treatment ends. But when it comes to it, when you have finished, perhaps the prospect doesn't seem so attractive after all.

For many people, the period immediately after treatment is marked by real feelings of vulnerability and of not wanting to stray too far from home or from the easy reach of medical and nursing care. Apart from the tiredness and fatigue, the feeling of not being entirely safe is powerful – powerful enough to spoil a holiday or break. There is also the sense that you cannot afford to look too far into the future, that planning too far ahead brings its own worries and fears.

Your time horizon has been understandably limited to the next treatment, the next clinic appointment. You may have been living one day at a time. To switch suddenly to planning six months ahead seems to be a task too much. I must say that I regard the point at which someone can look forward to and plan a holiday is a key sign of recovery. It doesn't always happen quickly, and often not as quickly as people might like, but happen it does. One of the things that I will advise people to do is to plan for short trips away – perhaps a couple of hours – to places they know and with which they are familiar. Once they can do that without too much anxiety, then perhaps a few trips for a bit longer but not staying away from home overnight just yet. When that is done to your satisfaction, you can plan to spend one night away – and not too far away – and so on, building up gradually, one step at a time. And that model is the key to many aspects of the rehabilitation programme that will rebuild both physical and emotional strength – one step at a time. It is much better to set yourself an easy target which you know you can achieve and end up saying to yourself 'That was easy, I could have done more of that' rather than going too far too fast and feeling that you have failed.

Breaking down all the tasks of living into easily manageable chunks – a step at a time – is a well tried and tested route to success. In our enthusiasm we often forget just how complex and difficult this life business is, and it's only when you have to get back on the roundabout that you realise this. Sometimes I think that living is like competing in an Olympic event but because we take it so much for granted we forget how demanding and tiring it can be, even at an ordinary, everyday level.

Let's take this analogy further and pretend that we are all Olympic sprinters – a rather far-fetched concept in my case, I should add – who have had a serious injury. We would not consider getting back to running the 100 metres until we have fully recovered. We would put ourselves on a gentle retraining programme, beginning with gentle walks rather than sprints. Getting back to living life should be done in the same way. A gentle build-up to the main event.

Of course one of the other factors contributing to lack of confidence is the uncertainty that living with cancer brings.

Living with uncertainty

This is one of the most difficult aspects of living with the aftermath of cancer. You will note that I have deliberately avoided using the phrase 'coming to terms with' uncertainty, because the reality is that this is something to be lived with and managed not 'come to terms with'. For those of us not living with this threat, this Sword of Damocles, truly understanding what it feels like is almost impossible. The nearest that I can get to it is to think about that phase so often used lightly and as banter – 'See you tomorrow unless I get run over by a bus'. The difference between those living with the threat of cancer returning and those free from it is that you have seen the bus coming and don't know whether it will stop in time. Until you can be given a 100% cast-iron, gold-plated, rock solid guarantee that your cancer is completely gone, never to return, then you will have that nagging worry gnawing away at you.

Again, immediately after treatment finishes, these fears may be at their worst, compounded by the lack of trust in your body and the lack of confidence that you may be feeling. It makes sense that you would feel that way and the reality and power of your feelings need to be acknowledged by all around you, both lay and professional. As time goes on, you may well find that the terrors inspired by the uncertainty reduce and are sent to the back of your mind rather than residing in its forefront. However, it may not take much to restore them – clinic visits, milestones and anniversaries, high profile celebrities with cancer – can all serve as potent reminders of what you have been through and may bring everything flooding back with a vengeance.

It would be surprising if this were not the case. Your experiences cannot be expunged or erased from your memory banks; they can be made less accessible, less easily revisited, but there they will be. It would be impossible to simply 'Put all that behind you and forget about it' as some of you may have been exhorted to do. If only it were as easy as that. What is often helpful, to balance your understandable pessimistic and frightening thoughts, is to remind yourself of any helpful comments that your doctors and nurses have made. These are constructive alternatives that are not about naively 'looking on the bright side' but are real counters to equally real fears. This brings me on to the next task.

Dealing with the world

You won't need me to tell you just how helpful a kindly word or supportive act can be. Likewise, you will need no reminders as to how hurtful and insensitive can be other words and comments. I have already quoted one phrase which I would class as not only impossible but also unhelpful and insensitive to boot – trying to 'forget all about it and put it all behind you'. This, of course, is often just what the person saying it to you wants to do and it can make for significant difficulties in communication if you want to talk about your worries whilst they want to act as if nothing happened. Although it is important to acknowledge other people's fears and anxieties which often provoke overly optimistic or excessively reassuring statements, that doesn't make them any easier to bear or tolerate.

It is quite probable that you will already have developed a mask that you put on in some situations in order to hide some of your real feelings. Most people need to defend themselves against the unwittingly hurtful or the crudely insensitive remark. Many of you will have learned to smile sweetly as someone says brightly to you 'My, you look really well' when you actually feel terrible. There will be times you will need to keep this defence going because people will still say unhelpful things. Most people think that cancer is like other illnesses – once treatment is completed, the disease is cured and then you are 'better'. As you know only too well, the situation with cancer is infinitely more complex than this simplistic analysis. As I said to you last time, you have a right to privacy (so you don't have to tell people everything) and you have a right to tell people what is helpful and what is hurtful. This can be a very difficult task with some people who will take offence very easily, but for your own protection, I think that it's worth it – because, in the words of the advert, you are worth it.

Regaining mastery and control
This is the final task which builds on all those tasks that I have outlined before. It is the alternative to getting back to normal, a place which I said could be rediscovered. You are in a new and sometimes frightening place where the old certainties and structures are gone and where you are having to look at the world afresh. This doesn't mean that you have to change everything; it may mean that you change nothing. One way of thinking about this is to use yet another analogy. Most of us have a sort of life plan more or less worked out. For some people this is a highly detailed route identifying what we will be doing and by when. For others of us it is a rather vague amble with the odd aspiration sketched in. But once you meet a life threat, somehow the map becomes less clear, sometimes even a blank. This is a terrifying experience – where do you go from here when you can't see the future? For some people this is a chance to review and reshape their life. The realisation that life is too short gives an opportunity to decide what you want your life to be about. And there is nothing stopping you saying that you want it to be about what it was about before. Or it can be about wanting to stop doing what you did and becoming the world bungee-jumping champion. Everyone will find their own route and their own path and it is for people like me to provide support and help during that process.

To summarise thus far, what I have tried to do is suggest that the end of treatment is the beginning of something else – a rebuilding process that needs to be managed and directed. Paradoxically, in psychological terms, this may be the most challenging and difficult time of all. It is a time of immense psychological vulnerability when people may feel that they have gone to pieces and simply cannot cope any more. So a word here about coping – a term as misused and burdensome as any. During treatment you deal with life as best you can because you have to. You may not be comfortable or find it easy, but manage you do. During this time, there is often a good deal of support – both formal and informal – available. You are also dealing with very obvious and tangible stresses. Then, all of a sudden, you are on your own with just as many threats but these threats are must less obvious and immediate. And very commonly, people find that when they can relax their guard a bit, let go of the reins, that's when they feel they can't cope, that they are going mad, not managing things. All this at a time when they, apparently, should be able to cope better because the stresses are less.

I have already argued that, in fact, the stresses are no less, but different. And because you may be exhausted and washed-out, your ability to mobilise yet more energy is compromised. And what makes it worse is that you may be allowing yourself to think more deeply about some of the things that you have been pushing to the back of your mind – particularly about the future and about trying to make some sense of what has happened to you. So there is often a sense of turmoil, a lack of coherence in your understanding of yourself and the world. In my view, this is the point at which the need for some sort of support and space in which to talk through some of these issues is at its peak. You may need some time to sit down with someone – it doesn't have to be someone like me, although it can be – someone you trust, to reflect on what you have been through and to begin to put it in its rightful place in your personal life history.

I have not spoken much about mood yet and how this is linked up with all the other factors. There is, as you might imagine, a complex relationship between mood and all the issues that I have referred to. If you are feeling low, you won't find it easy to do things, your self-confidence will be low and your level of self-criticism high. If you are unable to do things, this in turn will make you low, so you can easily get trapped in a downward spiralling vicious circle. But there are two sets of feelings that commonly arise at the time of treatment finishing which we need to talk about. The first of these is a sense of abandonment. This makes sense. After all, for many weeks, if not months, you will have been cared for by a large number of people, all of whom have your welfare and well-being at heart. You may have met other patients and relatives with whom you have been able to swap stories and get powerful support from someone who really understands. There has always been someone there to check out that little niggling pain or troublesome symptom. There has been a routine, a structure for you to trust in. Then all of a sudden, it goes. One of my patients described it like this: 'I got the impression of being balanced on a plank somewhere high up and with nothing to grab hold of. I felt as if I were about to fall off into some abyss.'

Such feelings of aloneness and abandonment are not in any way a criticism of the people who have been caring for you. It is simply a reflection of the fact that they now have to focus on those who are starting out on the process that you have completed. The second set of feelings that some people experience is a sense of disappointment that they don't feel more joy and happiness at the end of the treatment, but rather a sense of let down, anticlimax almost. This can be in marked contrast to what they might have expected.

How is it that expected happiness does not arise? There are a number of plausible explanations. One of these is that it hasn't actually finished as you may still be experiencing the effects of treatment, even though its delivery is complete. You may also be still visiting clinics for checkups. And I have already referred to the uncertainty and sense of threat that may continue well beyond the actual end of treatment. There is also the fact that you may be completely de-energised – plain exhausted – which does not leave any spare capacity for unrestrained ecstasy. In addition, you will have been looking forward to the absence of something unpleasant rather than the eager anticipation of the arrival of something pleasant. So I am not surprised at patients' surprise at their lack of elation as treatment finishes.

It isn't all doom and gloom and there will be times when you wake up feeling better than you did the day before and this slow process will gradually change until one day you wake up feeling so well that you realise just how awful it has been. Remember that for months you may have been having to live one day at a time under the most difficult and challenging circumstances. You may well have been unable to enjoy those things you usually like – your sense of taste and smell may have been affected, your desire for food undermined by nausea, your ability to go out limited by your lack of energy. But now you are freed up from the routine of treatment, from the more immediate and restrictive side-effects of that treatment, you can begin to move away into a different space. Again, I would emphasise the principle of one step at a time. It is important to build up gradually and by maximising your changes of success. Small, easily achievable targets and goals will be the building bricks of your success.

In closing, I want to try and bring some of these strands and themes together in a coherent framework. What I have tried to do is give a sense that the end of treatment can be as challenging a time as any that you experience. It is made more difficult by the profound physical and emotional assaults to which you have been subjected. And it is the time when the obvious sources of support are unavailable. I have argued that there is every reason for feeling frightened and out of control at this time. But what I have also tried to do is give a sense in which you can manage this process in a way that may avoid some of the pitfalls. Regaining and rebuilding your strength – both physical and emotional – is a task that I cannot emphasise enough. That is your foundation. And taking the time to reflect, either with someone or on your own, about where you want to go from here, can begin to give you the sense of mastery and control that you may have been denied during the treatment itself. One part of this is the process of putting the experience of cancer in its right place in your life. For months, it has dominated, been in control. Now is the time to begin the long, slow process of putting it in the right box in your life – not forgetting about it, not denying its importance or power, not pretending it didn't happen. It has to be incorporated into your own life pattern and experience in such a way as to not interfere and interrupt any more than it has to. You accommodate and assimilate it into yourself, not come to terms with it.

The reflective process may face you with choices about where to go from here. The exact path you choose (or the one that you have already chosen) is entirely a matter of personal choice and circumstance. Some of you will become stalwarts in the voluntary sector, helping others by running and managing support groups and becoming activists in cancer care and cancer politics; others will want to leave that part of their lives in a separate compartment and distance themselves from that experience. There may be constraints on what you can and cannot do, and that has to be built in. Running the London Marathon may not be everybody's dream and it may even be a physical impossibility. But there are other aspirations and hopes that you will have fostered during your life. This may be the time to review those and make some choices – some may remain dreams, some will be less important than before, some may take on a greater value, some will become a reality. They are yours and yours for the making. "

CANCER SUPPORT CENTRES

National Support Groups

Bowel Cancer Support Group
Irish Cancer Society
43/45 Northumberland Road
Dublin 4
Freephone: 1800 200 700
support@irishcancer.ie
www.cancer.ie

Brain Tumour Support Group
Medical Social Work Department
St. Luke's Hospital
Highfield Road
Rathgar
Dublin 6
Tel: 01 406 5163

CanTeen Ireland
Carmichael Centre
North Brunswick St.
Dublin 7
Tel: 01 872 2012
Freephone: 1800 200 700
info@canteen.ie
www.canteen.ie

I've Got What?!
C/O Cross Cause Charity Shop
Blackrock
Co Louth
Tel: 086 339 5690

Lakelands Area Retreat and Cancer
Centre (LARCC)
Ballinalack
Mullingar
Co Westmeath
Tel: 044 937 1971
Callsave: 1850 719 719
info@larcc.ie
www.larcc.ie

Lymphoma Support Ireland
Irish Cancer Society
43/45 Northumberland Road
Dublin 4
Freephone: 1800 200 700
info@lymphoma.ie
www.lymphoma.ie

Men Against Cancer
Irish Cancer Society
43/45 Northumberland Road
Dublin 4
Freephone: 1800 200 700
support@irishcancer.ie
www.cancer.ie

Newbridge Myeloma Support
Group
4 Belmont Green
Newbridge
Co Kildare
Tel: 087 233 7797
mymyeloma@gmail.com
www.mymyeloma.ie

Reach to Recovery
Irish Cancer Society
43/45 Northumberland Road
Dublin 4
Freephone: 1800 200 700
support@irishcancer.ie
www.cancer.ie

Lymphoedema Ireland
C/o Irish Cancer Society
43/45 Northumberland Road
Dublin 4
Freephone: 1800 200 700
www.lymphireland.com
info@lymphireland.com

St Luke's Breast Cancer Support
Group
Highfield Road
Rathgar, Dublin 6
Tel: 01 406 5163

Leinster Support Groups

Éist, Carlow Cancer Support Group
5 Mount Clare Court
Carlow
Tel: 085 144 05 10
ARC Cancer Support
65 Eccles Street, Dublin 7
Tel: 01 830 7333
info@arccancersupport.ie
www.arccancersupport.ie

ARC Cancer Support
559 South Circular Road
Dublin 8
Tel: 01 707 8880
Email: info@arccancersupport.ie
www.arccancersupport.ie

Balbriggan Cancer Support Group
73 Castleland
Parkview, Balbriggan
Co. Dublin
Tel: 086 164 2234

Brain Tumour Information &
Support Group
St Luke's Hospital
Highfield Road
Rathgar, Dublin 6
Tel: 01 406 5163

CanTeen Ireland
Carmichael Centre
North Brunswick St.
Dublin 7
Tel: 01 872 2012
Freephone: 1800 200 700
info@canteen.ie
www.canteen.ie

Psycho Oncology Department
St Vincent's University Hospital
Tel: 01 221 3317
www.stvincvents.ie

St Luke's Breast Cancer Support
Group
St Luke's Hospital
Highfield Road
Rathgar
Dublin 6
Tel: 01 4065000

Stillorgan Cancer Support
C/O 80 Marsham Court
Stillorgan, Co Dublin
Tel: 01 288 5725

Tallaght Cancer Support Group
Millbrook Lawns
Tallaght, Dublin 24
Tel: 087 217 6486

Dundalk Cancer Support Group
Philipstown
Hackballs Cross
Dundalk, Co. Louth
Tel: 086 107 4257

Gary Kelly Cancer Support Centre
George's St.
Drogheda, Co Louth
Tel: 041 980 5100 / 086 195 9864
services@gkcancersupport.com
www.gkcancersupport.com

I've Got What?!
C/O Cross Cause Charity Shop
Blackrock, Co Louth
Tel: 086 339 5690

Newbridge Myeloma Support
Group
4 Belmont Green
Newbridge
Co Kildare
Tel: 087 233 7797
mymyeloma@gmail.com
www.mymyeloma.ie

The Cúisle Centre
Block Road
Portlaoise
Co Laois
Tel: 057 868 1492
cuislecentre@eircom.net
www.cuislecentre.com

Dóchas Offaly Cancer Support
Téach Dóchas
Offaly St.
Tullamore
Co Offaly
Tel: 057 932 8268
dochasoffaly@eircom.net
www.dochasoffaly.ie

Midlands Myeloma Support
Group
C/O Rohdu
Tullamore General Hospital
Tullamore
Co. Offlay
Tel: 057 932 1501 ext 371
dochasoffaly@eircom.net
www.mymyeloma.ie

Lakelands Area Retreat and
Cancer Centre (LARCC)
Ballinalack
Mullingar
Co Westmeath
Tel: 044 937 1971
Callsave: 1850 719 719
info@larcc.ie
www.larcc.ie

HOPE Cancer Support Centre
22 Upper Weafer St.
Enniscorthy
Co Wexford
Tel: 053 923 8555
mary@hopesupportcentre.ie

Arklow Cancer Support Group
25 Kingshill
Arklow, Co Wicklow
Tel: 085 110 0066
arklowcancersupport@gmail.com

Bray Cancer Support Centre
36B Main Street
Bray, Co Wicklow
Tel: 01 286 6966
bcsc@iol.ie
www.braycancersupport.ie

Greystones Cancer Support
La Touché Place
Greystones, Co Wicklow
Tel: 01 287 1601
Email:
info@greystonescancersupport.com

Rathdrum Cancer Support Centre
36 Main St.
Rathdrum
Co Wicklow
Tel: 087 292 8660
www.rathcan@gmail.com

Wicklow Cancer Support
1 Mortons Lane
Wicklow
Tel: 087 691 4657 / 0404 32696
wicklowcancersupport@gmail.com

Munster Support Groups

Sláinte an Chláir
Tir Mhuire
Kilnamona
Co. Clare
Callsave: 1850 211 630
admin@clarecancersupport.com
www.clarecancersupport.com

Cork ARC Cancer Support House
Cliffdale
5 O'Donovan Rossa Road
Cork
Tel: 021 427 6688
karen@corkcancersupport.ie
ellen@corkcancersupport.ie
www.corkcancersupport.ie

Cancer Support - West Cork
Community Work Department
HSE
Skibereen
Co. Cork
Tel: 027 534 85 / 086 862 5417

Cúnamh Bon Secours Cancer
Support Group
St Bernadette's Corridor
Bon Secours Hospital
College Road
Cork
Tel: 021 480 1676
www.cunamh.ie

Youghal Cancer Support Group
161 North Main St.
Youghal
Co. Cork
Tel: 024 923 53

Kerry Cancer Support Group
Acorn Centre
47 Liosdara
Oakpark
Tralee, Co. Kerry
Tel: 087 230 8734
kerrycancersupportgroup@live.ie

Listowel Cancer Support
Group
Bedford
Listowel
Co. Kerry
Tel: 068 21 741 / 087 237 0766

Recovery Haven
5 Haig's Terrace
Tralee
Co. Kerry
Tel: 066 719 2122
recoveryhaven@gmail.com
www.recoveryhavenkerry.org

Cancer Information and
Support Centre
Mid-Western Regional
Hospital
Dooradoyle
Limerick
Tel: 061 485 163
www.midwesterncancercentre.ie

CARE Cancer Support Centre
14 Wellington Street
Clonmel
Co. Tipperary
Tel: 052 618 2667
caresupport@eircom.net
www.cancercare.ie

Suaimhneas Cancer Support
Centre
2 Clonaslee Gortlandroe
Nenagh
Co Tipperary
Tel: 067 37 403
suaimhneascancersupport
@eircom.net

Suir Haven Cancer Support
Clongour Road
Clongour
Thurles, Co. Tipperary
Tel: 0504 21 197
suirhaven@gmail.com

Solas Cancer Support Centre
Williamstown
Waterford
Tel: 051 87 6629
051-304604
info@solascentre.ie
www.solascentre.ie

Connaught Support Groups
Athenry Cancer Care
Social Service Centre
New Line Athenry
Co Galway
Tel:
091 84 4319 / 087 412 8080

Athlone Breast Cancer
Support Group
Tel: Jean 087-9593917
Email:
jeangough1@gmail.com

Ballinasloe Cancer Support Centre
Society St.
Ballinasloe
Co. Galway
Tel: 090 964 5574 / 087 945 2300
ballinasloecancer@yahoo.co.uk

CD's Helping Hands
Lakeview Point
Claregalway Corporate Park
Claregalway
Co Galway
Tel: 091 799 749
087 660 0103 (for emergency/after
hours calls)
info@cdshelpinghands.ie
www.cdshelpinghands.ie

Gort Cancer Support Group
The Hawthorn
Ennis Road
Gort, Co. Galway
Tel: 086 312 4220 / 086 172 4500

Tuam Cancer Care Centre
Cricket Court
Dunmore Road
Tuam, Co Galway
Tel: 093 28 522
Email: tccg@eircom.net
www.tuamcancercaregroup.ie

Cara Iorrais Cancer Support
Centre
2 Church St.
Belmullet
Co Mayo
Tel: 097 20 590
caraiorrais@gmail.com

Mayo Cancer Support Association
Rock Rose House
32 St Patrick's Avenue
Castlebar
Co Mayo
Tel: 094 903 8407
mayocancersupport@eircom.net
www.mayocancer.ie

Roscommon Cancer Support
Group
Vita House
Family Centre
Abbey St.
Roscommon
Tel: 090 662 5898
vitahouse@eircom.net

Sligo Cancer Support Centre
44 Wine St.
Sligo
Tel: 071 917 0399
scsc@eircom.net
www.sligocancersupportcentre.ie

Ulster Support Groups
Cootehill Community Cancer
Support Group
Cootehill
Co. Cavan
Tel: 087 622 0000

Yana Cancer Support Centre
Belturbet
Co. Cavan
Tel: 087 994 7360

Breast Centre Northwest
Letterkenny General Hospital
Letterkenny
Co. Donegal
Tel: 074 912 5888

Cancer Support and Social Club
Tiernaleague
Carandonagh
Co. Donegal
Tel: 086 602 8993 / 087 763 4596

Eist East Inishowen Cancer
Support Group
C/O Serenity House
2 Montgomery Terrace
Moville
Co Donegal
Tel: 074 938 2874

The Forge Cancer Support Group
The Forge Family Resource Centre
Pettigo
Co. Donegal
Tel: 071 986 1924

Good and New Drop In Centre
Unit 1
Portlink Business Park
Port Road
Letterkenny
Co Donegal
Tel: 074 911 3437

Killybegs Cancer Support Group
Kille
Kilgar
Co. Donegal
Tel: 074 973 12 92

Living Beyond Cancer
Oncology Day Services
Letterkenny General Hospital
Letterkenny
Co. Donegal
Tel: 074 912 5888 Bleep 674

Solace Donegal Cancer Support
Centre
St Joseph's Avenue
Donegal Town
Tel: 074 974 0837
solacedonegal@eircom.net

The following is a list of cancer support groups and centres that are not affiliated to the Irish Cancer Society. You may contact them directly for information regarding their services.

Cancer Care West
Costello Road
University College Hospital Galway
Tel: 091 545 000
info@cancercarewest.ie
www.cancercarewest.ie.

Limerick Cancer Support Group
Social Services Centre
Henry St.
Limerick
Tel: 061 337 528

Little Way Cancer Centre
4 Woods Way
College Road
Clane
Co. Kildare
Tel: 045 902 996

Carrickmacross Cancer
Society
Derryolam
Carrickmacross
Co. Monoghan
Tel: 087 753 5280

Information on the Comfort Fund – Marie Keating Foundation

Information on Travel2Care and Care to Drive – Irish Cancer Society

List of Cancer Support Centres – Irish Cancer Society

Every effort has been made to fulfil requirements with regard to reproducing copyright material. The author and publisher will be glad to rectify any omissions at the earliest opportunity.

1 800 200 700

Any question
on any cancer
from anybody
free of charge.
Mon-Thurs, 9am-7pm
Friday, 9am-5pm

REFERENCES

Books

Dr. Stephen & Gina Antczak, *Cosmetics Unmasked*, Thorsons, 2001

Dawn Mellowship, *Toxic Beauty*, Octopus Publishing Group Ltd., 2009

Sarah Stacey & Josephine Fairley, *The Green Beauty Bible*, Kyle Cathie Ltd., 2008

Katrina Ellis, *Shattering the Cancer Myth*, Hinkler Books Pty Ltd., 2003

Gene Spiller & Bonnie Bruce, *Cancer Survivors' Nutrition & Health Guide*, Prima Publishing, 1997

Shakti Gawain, *Creative Visualisation*. Nataraj Publishing, 2002

Alastair J. Cunningham, *The Healing Journey*, Healing. Journey Books, 2010

John O'Donohue, *Benedictus*, Transworld Publishers, 2007

Bernie Siegel, *Love, Medicine and Miracles*, Arrow Books, 1988

Websites

http://organicblog.wordpress.com

www.ewg.org

www.irishcancersociety.ie

www.cancer.gov

www.cancerselfcare.com

www.breastcancer.org

www.nwhealth.edu/healthyu/stayhealthy

www.chemocare.com

www.webMD

www.cincovidas.com

www.lymphireland.com

www.medicinenet.com

www.mldireland.com

www.trulife.com

nottheyearyouhadplanned.wordpress.com

How Can I Help Myself...

**If Somebody Offers Help,
What Would I Like Them To Do...**

What Helps Me To Relax...

What Inspires Me...
Words of Wisdom... People... Friends...

My Wish List...Dreams/Things I Would Like To Do...